Handbook for County Social Services Boards

2009

John L. Saxon

UNC
SCHOOL OF GOVERNMENT

THE UNIVERSITY
of NORTH CAROLINA
at CHAPEL HILL

The School of Government at the University of North Carolina at Chapel Hill works to improve the lives of North Carolinians by engaging in practical scholarship that helps public officials and citizens understand and improve state and local government. Established in 1931 as the Institute of Government, the School provides educational, advisory, and research services for state and local governments. The School of Government is also home to a nationally ranked graduate program in public administration and specialized centers focused on information technology, environmental finance, and civic education for youth.

As the largest university-based local government training, advisory, and research organization in the United States, the School of Government offers up to 200 courses, seminars, and specialized conferences for more than 12,000 public officials each year. In addition, faculty members annually publish approximately fifty books, book chapters, bulletins, and other reference works related to state and local government. Each day that the General Assembly is in session, the School produces the *Daily Bulletin*, which reports on the day's activities for members of the legislature and others who need to follow the course of legislation.

The Master of Public Administration Program is a full-time, two-year program that serves up to sixty students annually. It consistently ranks among the best public administration graduate programs in the country, particularly in city management. With courses ranging from public policy analysis to ethics and management, the program educates leaders for local, state, and federal governments and nonprofit organizations.

Operating support for the School of Government's programs and activities comes from many sources, including state appropriations, local government membership dues, private contributions, publication sales, course fees, and service contracts. Visit www.sog.unc.edu or call 919.966.5381 for more information on the School's courses, publications, programs, and services.

Michael R. Smith, DEAN
Thomas H. Thornburg, SENIOR ASSOCIATE DEAN
Frayda S. Bluestein, ASSOCIATE DEAN FOR PROGRAMS
Todd A. Nicolet, ASSOCIATE DEAN FOR OPERATIONS
Ann Cary Simpson, ASSOCIATE DEAN FOR DEVELOPMENT AND COMMUNICATIONS
Bradley G. Volk, ASSOCIATE DEAN FOR ADMINISTRATION

FACULTY

Gregory S. Allison
David N. Ammons
Ann M. Anderson
A. Fleming Bell, II
Maureen M. Berner
Mark F. Botts
Joan G. Brannon
Michael Crowell
Shea Riggsbee Denning
James C. Drennan
Richard D. Ducker
Robert L. Farb
Joseph S. Ferrell
Alyson A. Grine
Milton S. Heath Jr.
Norma Houston (on leave)
Cheryl Daniels Howell
Jeffrey A. Hughes

Joseph E. Hunt
Willow S. Jacobson
Robert P. Joyce
Kenneth L. Joyner
Diane M. Juffras
David M. Lawrence
Dona G. Lewandowski
James M. Markham
Janet Mason
Laurie L. Mesibov
Christopher B. McLaughlin
Kara A. Millonzi
Jill D. Moore
Jonathan Q. Morgan
Ricardo S. Morse
C. Tyler Mulligan
David W. Owens
William C. Rivenbark

Dale J. Roenigk
John Rubin
John L. Saxon
Jessica Smith
Karl W. Smith
Carl W. Stenberg III
John B. Stephens
Charles A. Szypszak
Shannon H. Tufts
Vaughn Upshaw
A. John Vogt
Aimee N. Wall
Jeffrey B. Welty
Richard B. Whisnant
Gordon P. Whitaker
Eileen R. Youens

Contents

Preface

Each year more than 400 citizens across North Carolina volunteer their time, energy, and talents to participate in county government as members of county social services boards. They come from almost every walk of life but have in common an unselfish commitment to public service. An invitation to serve on a county social services board is an honor and an expression of confidence, but it is also a request for a substantial commitment of time and energy.

This *Handbook for County Social Services Boards* provides board members with the information that they need to perform their public responsibilities lawfully and effectively, including information regarding the social services board's legal powers and duties; the roles and responsibilities of the board of county commissioners, the county social services director, the North Carolina General Assembly, the state Social Services Commission, and the state Department of Health and Human Services with respect to social services; the legal rules that govern the board's meetings and procedures; and the laws governing the administration and financing of public assistance and social services programs in North Carolina.

This handbook replaces a loose-leaf *Handbook for County Social Services Board Members* that was produced and distributed by the University of North Carolina at Chapel Hill's Institute (now School) of Government and the North Carolina Division of Social Services in 1992.

This handbook is supplemented by *Social Services in North Carolina* (published by the UNC School of Government in 2008). *Social Services in North Carolina* provides more detailed information on North Carolina's state-supervised and county-administered social services system; the roles and responsibilities of the federal, state, and local governments for the creation, administration, and financing of public assistance and social services programs; the organization and structure of state and county social services agencies; and related issues.

A shorter pamphlet, *Serving on the County Board of Social Services* (available on the School of Government's website at www.sog.unc.edu/pubs/electronicversions/pdfs/socservbds.pdf), is available for people who have been asked to serve on, or are seeking appointment to, the county social services board.

I would like to thank Janet Mason, my faculty colleague, mentor, and friend, who read the entire manuscript for this handbook and offered a number of valuable comments and helpful suggestions, as well as the other UNC faculty members—David Lawrence, Fleming Bell, Diane Juffras, Vaughn Upshaw, and Peg Carlson—and Drake Maynard and Keita Cannon in the North Carolina Office of State Personnel for their advice and assistance in reviewing particular parts of the manuscript. This handbook is better and more accurate because of their contributions.

It is my sincere hope that this handbook will be a useful resource for those civic-minded citizens who serve on North Carolina's county social services boards and that it will contribute to the School of Government's long and proud tradition of practical scholarship that seeks to improve the lives and well-being of North Carolinians by helping public officials and citizens better understand and improve state and local government.

John L. Saxon
Professor of Public Law and Government
School of Government
The University of North Carolina at Chapel Hill
Chapel Hill, North Carolina
May 2009

Chapter 1

Social Services in North Carolina

County social services boards in North Carolina function within a large and complex social services system. Therefore board members need at least a general understanding of the social services programs that are provided to county residents, the state and county social services agencies that administer those programs, and the roles and responsibilities of North Carolina counties, North Carolina's state government, and the federal government with respect to social services policy, administration, and funding.[1]

What Is "Social Services"?
In its broadest sense, social services refers to

- the broad array of services and assistance that public and private agencies provide to meet the social, economic, and human needs of children, families, senior citizens, disabled persons, and the poor;[2]
- the dozens of programs that are administered by state and county social services agencies and the assistance and services that are provided through these programs;

1

- the large and complex system of public and private agencies that establish, fund, supervise, and administer social services programs; and
- the intricate system of laws, policies, and procedures that govern social services agencies and programs.

For many years the term "welfare" was used to refer to government assistance and social services programs and to the public agencies that administered these programs. Over the past forty years, however, "social services" generally has replaced "welfare" in the law and public discourse. Today, social services programs that provide assistance to low-income individuals and families often are referred to as "public assistance," "means tested," or "safety net" programs—terms that generally do not carry the same social stigma as "welfare" and also reflect the U.S. Supreme Court's decisions holding that government assistance for the poor is, at least in some instances, a legal right or entitlement, not charity.[3] In addition, the change from "welfare" to "social services" reflects the fact that state and county social services agencies provide a range of social services for children, families, and the elderly (including adult and child protective services, adoption services, employment services, and child support enforcement services) as well as financial assistance or "welfare" payments for low-income individuals and families.

Negative public perceptions regarding "social services," however, persist.

Many people view social services programs as being too costly; there is inadequate awareness of what many of them actually accomplish; and biases and myths about [social services] programs and recipients continue to exist.[4]

In addition, the "complexity of the social services system and . . . [social services] programs . . . contributes to public misunderstanding" of social services.[5] Social services programs and agencies, therefore, continue to be "affected by shifts in the availability of private and charitable resources, economic conditions, and the political climate."[6]

Social Services Programs and Agencies

Broadly speaking, the goal of "social services" is to help children, families, the poor, disabled persons, and senior citizens achieve and maintain economic and social well-being.

This purpose is reflected in the mission statements adopted by many state and county social services agencies. For example, North Carolina's Division of Social Services defines its mission as

- ensuring that individuals and families have sufficient economic resources to obtain the basic necessities of life,
- assisting individuals in achieving and maintaining self-sufficiency through employment if possible,
- ensuring that children and adults are protected from abuse, neglect, and exploitation, and
- assisting disabled and dependent adults while ensuring that they live in the most independent setting feasible with the least possible intrusion from public agencies.[7]

In addition the objectives of particular social services programs often are reflected in statements of purpose contained in federal and state law. For example, federal law states that the purposes of the Temporary Assistance for Needy Families (TANF) program are to

- provide assistance to needy families so children may be cared for in their own homes or in the homes of relatives;
- end the dependence of needy parents on government benefits by promoting job preparation, work, and marriage;
- prevent and reduce the incidence of out-of-wedlock pregnancies; and
- encourage the formation and maintenance of two-parent families.[8]

Social services programs and agencies provide a "safety net" for children, families, the poor, disabled persons, and senior citizens by addressing a range of economic and social problems that impair the ability of those groups to function adequately in society. Such problems include poverty, hunger, and malnutrition; lack of medical care; homelessness; child abuse and neglect; elder abuse and neglect; teenage pregnancy; out-of-wedlock births; and unemployment. And, because these social problems affect the general welfare and well-being of the entire community, social services programs and agencies also serve the community, the county, and the state when they address the social, economic, and human needs of individuals and families.

To address these needs and problems, public social services agencies provide a range of assistance and services to children, families, the poor, disabled persons, and senior citizens. Some social services programs provide financial assistance, food, or health care to individuals and families with limited incomes. Others provide services to protect vulnerable children or adults from abuse or neglect, to collect child support from absent parents, or to help individuals or families become more self-sufficient.

County social services departments administer dozens of social services programs.[9] Each of these programs, however, has its own rules regarding eligibility, assistance, services, administration, and funding. And the rules that govern these programs are often incredibly detailed, complex, and confusing, filling hundreds of pages in social services policy and procedure manuals. Thus a person or family might be eligible for assistance under one program but ineligible for assistance under another. Some social services programs provide assistance only for children and families. Others serve only elderly or disabled persons. Some social services programs are "means tested" and provide assistance only to persons whose incomes and assets are low enough to be considered poor.[10] Other social services are not means tested and may be provided to individuals regardless of whether they are "poor."

North Carolina's Social Services System

North Carolina's social services system "is hard to summarize because it is so diverse and complex."[11]

In most states, social services programs are administered by state social services agencies—not by local governments—and are funded by federal and state tax revenues without local government funding.

North Carolina, by contrast, has adopted a "county-administered and state-supervised" system of social services under which

- social services programs are administered primarily by county social services agencies under the supervision of state social services agencies, and
- counties are required to pay part of the cost of social services programs.[12]

The social services system in North Carolina, therefore, involves "complicated relationships among the federal, state, and county governments."[13] All three levels of government—federal, state, and local—are involved in funding and administering social services programs. And at each of these levels of government, a number of agencies, boards, or commissions, as well as legislative or quasi-legislative bodies and (at the federal and state levels) the courts, exercise specific responsibilities in the creation, funding, supervision, or administration of social services programs. Responsibility for social services, therefore, is shared by the federal, state, and county governments and is exercised through a complex network of government agencies.

In some instances, one level of government exercises complete and exclusive responsibility with respect to a particular social services program, while the other two levels of government have little or no responsibility for that program. For example, the federal government is responsible for the administration and funding of the federal Supplemental Security Income (SSI) program. In other instances, responsibility for a particular social services program may be shared by two or three levels of government and by one or more branches, departments, or agencies at each level. For example, the federal government, the state, and counties each have certain administrative, fiscal, or policy-making responsibilities with respect to North Carolina's Medicaid program.

As a result, the state's social services system involves complicated, complex, and often overlapping and potentially conflicting relationships among and within the federal government, state government, and local governments.

The State's Role and Responsibilities

In North Carolina, the general role and responsibility of state government with respect to social services is spelled out in two sections of the North Carolina Constitution of 1970.

One of these provisions is similar to a section of the North Carolina Constitution of 1868. This provision recognizes the state's duty to provide "beneficent [care] for the poor, the unfortunate, and . . . orphan[s]."[14] The second provision requires the state to establish and operate, under such organization and in such manner as the North Carolina General Assembly may prescribe, "such charitable [and] benevolent . . . institutions and agencies as the needs of humanity and the public good may require."[15]

The North Carolina Constitution, therefore, recognizes the state's authority and responsibility to create, administer, and fund social services programs and agencies to provide assistance and services to needy families, children, and individuals. But it does not prescribe

- the extent and scope of the state's responsibility for social services,

- which social services agencies (other than a state board of public welfare) must be established,
- which social services programs must be created or funded,
- how state social services agencies must be organized, or
- how state social services programs must be administered or funded.

Under the constitutional provisions discussed above, the General Assembly is primarily responsible for determining the extent and scope of the state's responsibility for social services and how the state will discharge its responsibility.[16] To do so, the General Assembly[17] enacts legislation that

- creates and defines the responsibilities of state social services agencies;
- creates state social services programs;
- authorizes the state to participate in federal–state social services programs;[18]
- appropriates state funding for federal–state and state social services programs;
- allocates federal social services funds received by the state;
- determines how state social services programs will be administered and funded;
- approves the state's TANF plan;
- determines which counties will be designated as "electing" counties under the Work First (TANF) program;
- determines who is eligible for Medicaid and what services will be provided under the state's Medicaid program;
- determines local government's role, authority, and responsibility with respect to social services; and
- determines whether counties will be required to pay all or part of the nonfederal share of the cost of federal–state and state social services programs.

Much, but not all, of the social services legislation enacted by the General Assembly is codified in Chapter 108A of the North Carolina General Statutes (hereinafter G.S.), which includes laws regarding county administration of social services programs, administration of specific social services programs (such as Work First, State–County Special Assistance, Foster Care and Adoption Assistance, Food and Nutrition Services, Medicaid, Health Choice, and adult protective services), confidentiality of social services records, and financing of social services programs.[19]

The General Assembly also exercises general oversight authority over the state's social services agencies and programs by requiring the agencies to report to the General Assembly on a variety of subjects that involve the administration of social services programs.[20] And from time to time, the General Assembly authorizes studies of social services agencies and programs by the Legislative Research Commission, the Department of Health and Human Services, or other state study commissions.

As noted above, the North Carolina Constitution gives the General Assembly the authority to establish state agencies and institutions to "serve the needs of humanity and the public good."[21] Acting pursuant to this authority, the General Assembly has created the state Department of Health and Human Services (DHHS) and has designated DHHS as the single state agency that is responsible for administering or supervising the administration of state and federal–state social services programs.[22]

Under North Carolina's county-administered and state-supervised social services system, DHHS and its constituent divisions are primarily responsible for the supervision of state and federal–state social services programs. DHHS, however, is responsible, directly or through contracts with private vendors, for some administrative functions, such as paying Work First Family Assistance benefits, processing and paying Medicaid claims, determining disability for the state's Medicaid program, operating the child support enforcement program in twenty-nine of the state's counties, and hearing and deciding administrative appeals involving eligibility for social services programs.

DHHS and the Social Services Commission also are authorized under state law to adopt administrative rules and regulations regarding social services programs. These administrative rules, however, must be consistent with applicable state statutes and adopted in accordance with the state's Administrative Procedure Act.[23]

The Counties' Role and Responsibilities

Although the North Carolina Constitution speaks of the state's responsibility for social services, the state may delegate all or part of its responsibility for social services to counties.[24]

North Carolina's one hundred counties are political subdivisions of the state. Counties have no inherent powers of self-government. Instead they may exercise only those powers conferred on them by state law and must exercise those powers, duties, and responsibilities that are imposed on them by state law.[25] So the counties' role and responsibilities with respect to social services in North Carolina are based on state laws that authorize or require counties to administer or fund social services programs.

As noted above, under North Carolina's state-supervised and county-administered social services system, county social services agencies are primarily responsible for administering state and federal–state social services programs under the supervision of state social services agencies. Under this system, local social services agencies are part of county, not state, government, and employees of local social services agencies are county, not state, employees. County social services agencies, however, must comply with applicable state and federal requirements in administering state and federal–state social services programs.

In addition, North Carolina's county–state social services system requires counties to pay at least part of the cost of administering most state and federal–state social services programs and part of the cost of assistance and services provided under many state and federal–state social services programs.

North Carolina's state-supervised and county-administered system of social services reflects the state's long history of county responsibility for social services, the continuing role of counties as a primary means for providing basic government services to North Carolinians, and the strength of local government in North Carolina. But it also "represents an exception to the trend . . . to centralize at the state level the administration and funding of major government functions."[26] And the state's delegation to counties of administrative and fiscal responsibility for social services programs continues to generate some special problems and frustrations, as evidenced by recent debates regarding the fiscal impact of Medicaid on low-wealth counties.

The general parameters of the state–county relationship with respect to social services and the authority and responsibility of North Carolina counties for social services are set forth in several provisions of North Carolina's General Statutes.

G.S. 108A-1 requires every county in North Carolina to have a county board of social services (or in a county with a population of at least 425,000, a county social services board, a board of county commissioners that exercises the powers and duties of a county social services board, or a consolidated human services board). Similarly G.S. 108A-12 requires every county social services board to appoint a county social services director who is responsible for appointing the staff of the county department of social services, for administering state and federal–state social services programs as required by law, and for acting as the agent of the state DHHS.[27]

G.S. 153A-255 authorizes counties to undertake, sponsor, organize, engage in, and support any social service program that will further the health, welfare, education, employment, safety, comfort, and convenience of its citizens.[28] State law also requires counties or county departments of social services to administer, or to assist in the administration of, a number of state and federal–state social services programs, including Medicaid,[29] TANF[30] Food and Nutrition Services (Food Stamps),[31] Low-Income Energy Assistance,[32] State–County Special Assistance,[33] Foster Care and Adoption Assistance,[34] child protective services,[35] adult protective services,[36] guardianship services,[37] Health Choice,[38] and child support enforcement services.[39]

State law, however, also requires counties to administer state and federal–state social services programs in accordance with applicable requirements set forth in federal and state law and rules and under the supervision of the state DHHS.[40] And in at least one instance, state law expressly addresses the state's authority to supervise, direct, and control the county's provision of social services. G.S. 108A-74 allows the state to impose a corrective action plan on a county, to withhold federal and state funding for the administration of child welfare services, or to take control of a county's child welfare program and provide these child welfare services through direct administration by the state DHHS or through contracts with other public or private agencies if a county department of social services fails to provide child protective services, foster care services, or adoption services in accordance with applicable state laws and regulations.

G.S. 153A-257 allocates responsibility for social services among the state's counties based on the "legal residence" of persons who are entitled to public assistance or social services.[41] If two or more county departments of social services disagree with respect to a minor's residence in a child abuse, neglect, or dependency case, the DHHS's Division of Social Services may determine which county is responsible for providing protective services and financial support for the minor.[42]

State law also provides that the General Assembly may divide the nonfederal share of the cost of social services for county residents between the state and counties.[43] When state law or rules require counties to pay part of the nonfederal share of social services programs, G.S. 108A-90 requires boards of county commissioners to levy and collect property taxes in an amount sufficient to pay the county share. If a county fails to pay its full share of social services costs to the state, the state may withhold from the county any state social services funding or sales tax revenues that otherwise would be paid to the county by the state.[44]

North Carolina counties, therefore, have a substantial amount of responsibility for the administration and funding of state and federal–state social services programs. In many instances this responsibility is discharged through the county department of social services under the supervision of the county social services director. In other instances responsibility rests with the county social services board or the board of county commissioners. In every instance, however, the authority and responsibility of counties, county commissioners, county social services departments, county social services directors, and county social services boards ultimately is defined by and subject to state law, state supervision, and state control.

The Federal Government's Role and Responsibilities

The U.S. Constitution allows, but does not require, the federal government to use federal tax revenues to establish and administer, or to assist state and local governments in administering, social services programs for the poor, the disabled, the elderly, and children.[45] Thus, unlike North Carolina's state government, the federal government does not have any constitutional obligation or responsibility to establish, administer, or fund social services programs. But it does have the legal authority to do so.

Responsibility for federal social services policy and law is vested primarily in the U.S. Congress, which enacts legislation creating federal and federal–state social services programs.[46] Federal social services statutes enacted by Congress determine the nature and scope of the federal government's role and responsibility for social services, which federal social services programs and agencies will be established, whether federal social services programs will be administered by federal social services agencies or through state or local social services agencies, how much the federal government will spend for federal social services programs, who will be eligible to receive assistance or services under these programs, what requirements will apply to federal social services funding provided to state or local social services agencies, and how much flexibility states will have in administering federal–state social services programs. These federal social services statutes generally specify the persons who are eligible to receive assistance or services under each federal or federal–state social services program, specify the type of assistance or services that may be provided under each program, specify how each program will be funded, and specify who will be responsible for administering each program. Congress also exercises primary fiscal authority for federal and federal–state social services programs by determining, through the federal budget and appropriations process, how much the federal government will spend on social services programs.

At the federal level, administrative responsibility for federal and federal–state social services programs is exercised by the U.S. Department of Health and Human Services and other federal departments, agencies, bureaus, and offices.

Some federal social services programs are administered directly by federal agencies. The federal Social Security Administration, for example, administers the Old Age, Survivors, and Disability Insurance (OASDI or Social Security) program and the SSI program. State and local governments have little or no responsibility for these federal programs. Other federal social services programs are administered primarily through private contractors. The federal Medicare program, for example, is administered by private health insurance carriers (like Blue Cross and Blue Shield) under the supervision of the Center for Medicare and Medicaid Services.

But many federal social services programs (or, more accurately, federal–state social services programs), including the Medicaid, Food Stamp, TANF, Low-Income Energy Assistance, Foster Care and Adoption Assistance, and child protective services programs, are administered by state and local social services agencies under the supervision of the U.S. Department of Health and Human Services or other federal agencies, which generally are responsible for

- reviewing and approving the social services plans that states submit to the federal government as a condition of receiving federal funding for these federal–state social services programs;
- distributing federal social services funding to states;
- issuing rules, regulations, and policies governing the states' administration of federally-funded social services programs;
- collecting and analyzing data with respect to these programs;
- monitoring the states' compliance with federal law, regulations, policies, and requirements that apply with respect to these programs; and
- withholding federal funds or imposing other penalties or sanctions when states fail to comply with federal requirements.

The relationship between the federal government and states with respect to these federal–state social services programs sometimes is described as one of "cooperative federalism." The nature and terms of this cooperative federal–state relationship vary from program to program and are spelled out in the requirements and conditions of applicable federal laws and regulations; in the provisions of the "state plan" for each program; and in the terms of federal grants, contracts, waivers, or agreements with the state. Generally, however, cooperative federalism means that the federal government

- pays all or part of the cost of federal–state social services programs;
- establishes some or all of the policies governing these programs; and
- allows states to administer these programs in accordance with federal requirements regarding eligibility, assistance, and program administration.[47]

Federal law, for example, requires that most federal–state social services programs be administered

- by a single state agency or by local social services agencies under the supervision of a single state agency;
- in all political subdivisions of the state under uniform, statewide policies;
- in a way that protects the legal rights and confidentiality of persons applying for or receiving assistance or services; and
- by employees who are selected and protected under a merit-based personnel system.

Some federal social services laws require states to pay part of the cost of federal–state social services programs based on federal match or maintenance of effort formulas. And federal social services laws often specify

- who is eligible or ineligible for assistance and services under federal–state social services programs,
- what type of assistance must or may be provided to eligible persons,
- how much assistance must or may be provided, and
- how long assistance or services must or may be provided.

These federal requirements often are called federal mandates. Strictly speaking, however, the federal government does not mandate or require any state to participate in or administer any federal–state social services program. Instead, federal social services mandates are more properly characterized as "strings" that are attached to federal social services funding, which is the "carrot" offered to induce states to participate in federal–state social services programs. North Carolina and other states, therefore, may decline to participate in any federal–state social services program and refuse to accept federal social services funding. But if the state chooses to participate in a federal–state social services program and to accept social services funding, it must comply with the federal requirements that are attached to the program and funding. And because states are required to comply with these federal requirements as a condition of receiving federal social services funding, these federal "mandates" affect and help shape state social services policies in an indirect, but nonetheless real, way.

There is no direct relationship between the federal government and counties with respect to federal–state social services programs. Instead the federal government provides funding for these programs to each state—not directly to counties—and holds the state, rather than counties, accountable for complying with federal requirements and conditions. Federal social services mandates, however, affect the administration and funding of federal–state social services programs at the local level because the federal mandates that are imposed on the state are passed on to counties along with federal funding for social services programs.

Notes

1. North Carolina's social services system is discussed in more detail in John L. Saxon, *Social Services in North Carolina* (Chapel Hill: School of Government, The University of North Carolina at Chapel Hill, 2008). The information in this chapter is primarily based on Chapters 1 and 3 of Saxon, *Social Services in North Carolina*.

2. The term "human services" is sometimes used to refer to these services. In this context, the term human services includes not only the public assistance and social services provided by state and county social services agencies but also clinical health services provided by public health departments; mental health, developmental disability, and substance abuse services provided through area mental health authorities; and a variety of other services (including homeless shelters, domestic violence prevention, housing assistance, child development, and services for children, youth, and senior citizens) that are provided by public and private agencies to meet the needs of families, children, youth, senior citizens, and others.

3. *See* Goldberg v. Kelly, 397 U.S. 254 (1970).

4. Mason P. Thomas Jr., and Janet Mason, *A Guidebook to Social Services in North Carolina,* 4th ed. (Chapel Hill: Institute of Government, The University of North Carolina at Chapel Hill, 1989), 1. Government programs for the poor have always raised public

concern regarding personal responsibility versus social responsibility, government responsibility versus private-sector responsibility, costs, fiscal accountability, fraud, and distinctions between those who are "deserving" of assistance and those who are not.

5. *Id.* at 1.

6. *Id.* at 1–2.

7. N.C. Division of Social Services website (www.dhhs.state.nc.us/dss/about/mission .htm).

8. 42 U.S.C. § 601.

9. North Carolina's public assistance and social services programs are summarized in Chapter 11 of Saxon, *Social Services in North Carolina*.

10. The federal poverty level (FPL) provides one measure, but not the only measure, for determining whether an individual or family is poor. The FPL is established by the U.S. Department of Health and Human Services (DHHS), is adjusted each year, varies based on the number of persons in the household, and attempts to provide a rough measure of the income a family needs in order to obtain adequate housing, food, and other necessities. In 2009 the FPL for a family of three living in North Carolina was $18,310 per year. In some instances, a family may be eligible for public assistance even if its income exceeds the FPL. But in other instances, a family cannot qualify for public assistance even though its income is below the FPL.

11. Mason P. Thomas Jr., *A Guidebook to Social Services in North Carolina,* 3d ed. (Chapel Hill: Institute of Government, The University of North Carolina at Chapel Hill, 3d ed. 1976), [i].

12. Public funding for social services programs is discussed in detail in Chapter 12 of Saxon, *Social Services in North Carolina*.

13. Thomas and Mason, *A Guidebook to Social Services in North Carolina*, 1.

14. N.C. Const. art. XI, §4.

15. N.C. Const. art. XI, §3.

16. *See* Martin v. Wake County, 208 N.C. 354, 180 S.E. 777 (1935) (care of indigent sick and afflicted poor is a proper function of state government, but the General Assembly may require counties, as administrative agencies of the state, to perform this function within their territorial limits); James Walker Mem'l Hosp. v. City of Wilmington, 237 N.C. 179, 74 S.E.2d 749 (1953); Craven County Hosp. Corp. v. Lenoir County, 75 N.C. App. 453, 331 S.E.2d 690 (1985); Rosie J. v. N.C. Dep't of Human Res., 347 N.C. 247, 491 S.E.2d 535 (1997) (the General Assembly's restrictions on the funding of medically necessary abortions for indigent women did not violate the state's constitutional obligations to provide beneficent care for the poor).

17. Within the General Assembly, the House Appropriations Subcommittee on Health and Human Services, Senate Appropriations Committee for Health and Human Services, House Committee on Children, Youth, and Families, and the Senate Committee on Mental Health and Youth Services exercise primary responsibility for proposed legislation regarding social services programs and agencies.

18. *See* N.C. GEN. STAT. § 108A-71 (hereinafter G.S.). The state's authority to adopt policies governing eligibility and benefits with respect to federal–state social services programs, such as the Food Stamp, Temporary Assistance for Needy Families (TANF), and

Medicaid programs, is limited by federal law and regulations. Federal law and regulations, however, give the state significant policy-making authority with respect to the Medicaid and TANF programs.

19. Other laws regarding social services agencies, employees, and programs are codified in Chapter 7B (Juvenile Code), Chapter 48 (Adoption), Chapter 110 (Child Welfare), Chapter 126 (State Personnel Act), and Chapter 153A (Counties) of the General Statutes. Social services policies adopted by the General Assembly also are included in uncodified session laws, such as uncodified provisions of the state's biennial appropriations act, which specifies who is eligible for Medicaid and what services will be provided under the state's Medicaid program. The state's biennial appropriations act also allocates federal funding that is received by the state under the Social Services Block Grant, the TANF Block Grant, the Child Care and Development Block Grant, and the Low-Income Energy Assistance Block Grant, and appropriates money from the state's General Fund for social services agencies and programs.

20. The General Assembly abolished the Joint Legislative Public Assistance Commission in 2001. S.L. 2001-424, sec. 21.13(a) (repealing G.S. 120-225).

21. N.C. Const. art. XI, § 3.

22. G.S. 108A-71; G.S. Ch. 143B, Art. 3.

23. G.S. Ch. 150B, Art. 2A. Administrative rules adopted by DHHS and the Social Services Commission are published in the North Carolina Register and codified in Title 10A of the North Carolina Administrative Code.

24. *See* Martin v. Wake County, 208 N.C. 354, 180 S.E. 777 (1935) (care of indigent sick and afflicted poor is a proper function of state government, but the General Assembly may require counties, as administrative agencies of the state, to perform this function within their territorial limits); James Walker Mem'l Hosp. v. City of Wilmington, 237 N.C. 179, 74 S.E.2d 749 (1953); Craven County Hosp. Corp. v. Lenoir County, 75 N.C. App. 453, 331 S.E.2d 690 (1985).

25. Duties that are imposed on counties by state law are called state mandates.

26. Janet Mason and John Saxon, "Social Services," in *State and Local Government Relations in North Carolina*, ed. Charles D. Liner, 2d ed. (Chapel Hill: Institute of Government, The University of North Carolina at Chapel Hill, 1995), 199. During the 1930s, North Carolina's state government assumed primary responsibility for funding the operation of public schools and for administering and funding prisons, roads, and highways. The state also assumed some additional responsibility for social services programs following enactment of the federal Social Security Act, but required counties to administer and pay part of the cost of most of the public assistance programs established under the Social Security Act. Since then, the state has significantly increased its administrative and fiscal responsibility for social services programs, but continues to administer most social services programs through county social services agencies and to require counties to pay part of the cost of state and federal–state social services programs.

27. G.S. 108A-14(2), (3), (5).

28. *See* 40 Op. N.C. Att'y. Gen. 704 (1969). *Cf.* Hughey v. Cloninger, 297 N.C. 86, 253 S.E.2d 898 (1979); Stam v. State, 302 N.C. 357, 275 S.E.2d 439 (1981).

29. G.S. 108A-25(b); G.S. 153A-255.

30. G.S. 108A-27(f), (g); G.S. 153A-255.

31. G.S. 108A-25(a)(3); G.S. 108A-51; G.S. 153A-255.

32. G.S. 108A-25(a)(5); G.S. 153A-255.

33. G.S. 108A-25(a)(2); G.S. 108A-40; G.S. 153A-255.

34. G.S. 108A-25(a)(4); G.S. 153A-255.

35. G.S. 7B-302.

36. G.S. 108A-103.

37. G.S. 108A-15; G.S. 153A-255.

38. G.S. 108A-70.26(a); G.S. 153A-255.

39. G.S. 110-141.

40. *See* G.S. 108A-1, G.S. 108A-14(3), G.S. 108A-25.

41. A person's legal residence generally is in the county in which he or she resides. A minor's legal residence generally is that of the parent or other relative with whom the minor resides. A person who is in a hospital, mental institution, nursing home, adult care home, group home, foster home, confinement facility, or similar institution does not necessarily reside in the county in which the institution is located.

42. G.S. 153A-257(d).

43. G.S. 108A-87.

44. G.S. 108A-93.

45. Article I, section 8, of the United States Constitution authorizes Congress to impose taxes and spend money to provide for the general welfare of the United States. The constitutionality of the federal government's authority to establish and fund social services programs was first upheld by the U.S. Supreme Court in 1937. *See* Helvering v. Davis, 301 U.S. 619 (1937).

46. Congress shares policy-making responsibility with the president, who may call on Congress to enact social services legislation or veto social services statutes passed by Congress; with federal agencies, which may adopt rules or regulations supplementing or implementing federal social services statutes; and with state governments, which may enact laws or adopt policies for some federal–state social services programs within the parameters set by Congress.

47. It is important to note that the federal government also gives states some discretion with respect to the operation of some federal–state social services programs, as long as that discretion is exercised within the parameters of federal requirements. For example, federal law generally provides that families may not receive TANF for more than sixty months, but allows states to adopt more stringent time limits or to allow a limited number of families to exceed the federal time limit. Similarly, the federal Medicaid statute requires states to cover certain categories of people and to provide certain medical services but gives states the option to cover other categories of people, to provide optional medical services, to determine the amount, scope, and duration of covered services, and to determine payment rates for covered services. Federal mandates, therefore, do not dictate every aspect of every federal–state social services program.

Chapter 2

History of County Social Services Boards

County social services boards have played an important role in the governance and administration of social services agencies and programs in North Carolina for almost a century.

County Boards of Charities and Public Welfare: 1917–1941

County social services boards were first established around 1917, following the General Assembly's enactment of a statute creating North Carolina's first statewide system of public welfare and social services.

Under the 1917 public welfare law, the board of county commissioners in each North Carolina county was authorized (but not required) to appoint a three-member county "board of charities and public welfare."[1] In 1919 the public welfare law was amended to require the appointment of a county board of charities and public welfare for each county.[2]

These county boards of charities and public welfare were the direct ancestors of today's county boards of social services.

Under the 1917 law, all three members of the county board of charities and public welfare were appointed by the board of county commissioners with the advice and consent of the state Board of Charities and Public Welfare (now the state Social Services Commission).[3] In 1919 the General Assembly amended the state's public welfare law to require that all three members of county boards of charities and public welfare be appointed directly by the state Board of Charities and Public Welfare.[4] Thus from 1919 until 1937, boards of county commissioners had no direct voice in the appointment of county social services boards. In 1937 the law was amended again to provide that one member of the county board of charities and public welfare would be appointed by the board of county commissioners, one member would be appointed by the state Board of Charities and Public Welfare, and the third member would be selected by the other two members of the county welfare board.[5]

County Public Welfare Boards: 1941–1969

Until 1941 county boards of social services were called county boards of charities and public welfare. In 1941 the name of these boards was changed to county public welfare boards.[6]

Before 1963 county welfare boards generally were comprised of three members.[7] In 1963 North Carolina's social services law was amended to allow boards of county commissioners to increase the size of their county's welfare board from three to five members (two members appointed by the board of county commissioners, two members appointed by the state's Social Services Commission, and one member selected by the other four county welfare board members).[8] Today almost all North Carolina counties have five-member social services boards; only a few counties still have three-member boards.

County Social Services Boards: 1969–1996

In 1969 the General Assembly changed the name of county welfare boards to county boards of social services.[9]

In 1973 the General Assembly enacted a statute, now codified as Section 153A-77 of the North Carolina General Statutes (hereinafter G.S.), authorizing the board of county commissioners in counties with populations of more than 325,000 (at that time, only Mecklenburg County) to assume and exercise the powers and duties of the county board of social services and of the county public health board and the county mental health board.[10]

In 1995 the General Assembly considered, but did not enact, legislation that would have made G.S. 153A-77 applicable to all North Carolina counties regardless of population.[11]

In 1996 the General Assembly amended G.S. 153A-77 to allow the governance of social services programs in counties with populations of more than 425,000 through

- the county board of social services,
- the board of county commissioners, or
- a consolidated county human services board.

Evolution of the Board's Role and Responsibilities

Until the 1960s county social services boards exercised a significant amount of authority and responsibility with respect to administering and establishing policies for public assistance and social services programs in North Carolina. For example, until 1953 the county welfare board had the exclusive authority to approve or deny all applications for old-age assistance and aid to dependent children (subject to eligibility requirements established by state law) and to determine the amount of assistance provided to elderly persons and children under these programs (subject to maximum payment amounts established by state law and subject to review by the board of county commissioners).[12]

The amount of authority and discretion exercised by county social services boards before the 1960s reflects the fact that during this period

- county social services departments administered fewer public assistance and social services programs than they do today,
- fewer people received public assistance and social services than today,
- the number of staff employed by county social services departments was far smaller than today, and
- the state and federal governments exercised far less control and supervision with respect to social services programs than they do today.

Since the 1960s, however, the number, scope, size, and complexity of public assistance and social services programs have grown dramatically; the size and professionalism of county social services staffs have increased; and the responsibility and authority of the federal and state governments with respect to social services programs have grown relative to that of counties. As a result responsibility and authority with respect to many aspects of social services programs have shifted more or less steadily over time from the county board of social services to the county director of social services, to state social services agencies, and to the federal government.[13]

Today social services boards are rarely involved in the administration of social services programs. Instead, the role of the county social services board primarily focuses on the general direction, oversight, and supervision of the county social services department.

The North Carolina Association of County Boards of Social Services

The North Carolina Association of County Boards of Social Services (NCACBSS) is a voluntary, nongovernmental association.

The mission of NCACBSS is to inform, educate, and empower county social services boards and social services board members; to serve as an advocate for the interests of county social services boards, departments, employees, and clients at the county, state, and federal levels of government; to increase public understanding, acceptance, and support of social services programs in North Carolina; and to promote closer working relationships between county social services boards and boards of county commissioners, the state Department of Health and Human Services, and other public and private human services agencies and associations.

The association publishes a newsletter and maintains a website (www .ncacbss.org) for members, helps plan statewide education and training programs and conferences for county social services board members, and participates in several statewide human services coalitions and advocacy groups.

The association is governed by a board of directors that consists of a president, secretary, treasurer, and regional directors elected by the association's members. The association's annual business meeting generally is held each fall in conjunction with the annual Social Services Institute (an annual conference and training program that is sponsored by the North Carolina Association of County Directors of Social Services).

Membership in the association is open to anyone who is a member of a county social services board and to former county social services board members who continue to participate in the association's activities.

Notes

1. 1917 N.C. Pub. Laws ch. 170 [Rev. (1905) §§ 3915, 3921].

2. 1919 N.C. Pub. Laws ch. 46, § 2 [Rev. (1905) § 3915].

3. 1917 N.C. Pub. Laws ch. 170 [Rev. (1905) § 3915].

4. 1919 N.C. Pub. Laws ch. 46, § 2 [Rev. (1905) § 3915]. The 1919 statute also expanded the powers and duties of the county boards of charities and public welfare.

5. 1937 N.C. Pub. Laws ch. 319, § 3 [C.S. § 5014]. A 1941 statute provided that the third member of Wake County's welfare board would be appointed by Raleigh's city council. 1941 N.C. Pub. Laws ch. 270, § 2 (C.S. § 5014).

6. 1941 N.C. Pub. Laws ch. 270, § 2 (C.S. § 5014).

7. Special legislation established five-member welfare boards in Guilford, Gaston, and Stokes counties. 1955 N.C. Sess. Laws ch. 312; 1957 N.C. Sess. Laws ch. 1157; 1963 N.C. Sess. Laws ch. 835.

8. 1963 N.C. Sess. Laws ch. 247 [N.C. GEN. STAT. § 108-11 (hereinafter G.S.)]. Between 1963 and 1969, the law did not apply to Cabarrus, Pender, Gaston, Columbus, Alexander, Chatham, Burke, Mitchell, or Watauga counties. In 1981 the General Assembly enacted a special local statute authorizing Mecklenburg County's board of commissioners to expand the size of the county's social services board, to determine the size of the expanded social services board, to determine the terms of social services board members, and to appoint all but two of the members of the county social services board. 1981 N.C. Sess. Laws ch. 625.

9. 1969 N.C. Sess. Laws ch. 546 (G.S. 108-7).

10. 1973 N.C. Sess. Laws ch. 454. The law was amended in 1985 to make it applicable to counties with populations of more than 400,000. The law was amended again in 1987 to make it applicable to counties with populations of more than 425,000. From 1973 until about 1991, Mecklenburg County was the only North Carolina county whose population exceeded the threshold established by G.S. 153A-77. From the early 1990s through 2000, Mecklenburg and Wake counties were the only counties whose populations exceeded the threshold established by G.S. 153A-77. G.S. 153A-77, however, probably applies now to Guilford County (with an estimated population of 460,780 as of July 2007) as well as to Mecklenburg and Wake counties (with populations of more than 800,000).

11. Senate Bill 468 (1995); House Bill 875 (1995).

12. 1937 N.C. Pub. Laws ch. 288, §§ 15, 45 [G.S. 108-30, 108-59 (1952)]. The 1937 public assistance law also authorized the board of county commissioners to review the county welfare board's actions with respect to applications for old-age assistance and aid to dependent children. 1937 N.C. Pub. Laws ch. 288, §§ 16, 46 [G.S. 108-31, 108-60 (1952)].

13. With the enactment of federal and state welfare reform laws in 1996 and 1997, North Carolina counties were given increased authority and flexibility with respect to administering, financing, and establishing policies for North Carolina's Work First (Temporary Assistance to Needy Families) program. State law, however, delegated most of this increased authority and flexibility to boards of county commissioners rather than to county boards of social services.

Chapter 3

The Board's Role, Size, Composition, and Legal Status

State law requires that each of North Carolina's one hundred counties establish a county board of social services (or, in the case of a county with a population of more than 425,000, that the board of county commissioners exercise the legal powers and duties that would otherwise be exercised by the county social services board, or establish a county human services board in lieu of county boards for social services, public health, and mental health, developmental disability, and substance abuse services).[1] State law also specifies the role and responsibilities of county social services boards and governs the size and composition of those boards.

Role and Responsibilities of the County Social Services Board

The primary role of the county social services board is to provide effective, responsible, and accountable public oversight and direction of the county social services department and to advise local government officials with respect to the development of policies and plans to improve social conditions in the county.

In order for social services boards to fulfill this role, state law authorizes them to exercise a number of specific powers and duties, including

- appointing the county director of social services (following the rules and procedures set forth by the State Personnel Act and the State Personnel Commission);[2]
- consulting with and advising the director;[3]
- evaluating the director's performance;
- disciplining or dismissing the director if the director engages in unacceptable personal conduct or the director's job performance is unsatisfactory (in accordance with the rules and procedures established by the State Personnel Act and the State Personnel Commission);
- assisting the director in preparing a proposed social services budget and transmitting the proposed social services budget to the board of county commissioners;[4]
- establishing local policies for public assistance and social services programs (which must be consistent with federal and state social services laws, rules, and policies);[5]
- advising county and municipal authorities with respect to the development of policies and plans to improve the social conditions of the community;[6] and
- exercising such other powers and duties as the General Assembly, the state Social Services Commission, the state Department of Health and Human Services (DHHS), or the board of county commissioners may assign.[7]

In exercising these powers and duties, social services boards perform a variety of functions, including oversight, direction, supervision, evaluation, advice and consultation, advocacy, public education, community relations, public representation and accountability, strategic planning, management and administration, policy-making, quasi-judicial decision-making, public leadership, and governance.

Social services boards, therefore, play a significant role with respect to the county social services department and the social services it provides to county residents. The boards do not, however, have exclusive, overall, primary, or ultimate responsibility with respect to the county social services department or the provision of social services to county residents and must exercise their legal authority within the parameters set by state law.

Size and Composition of Social Services Boards

County social services boards consist of either three or five members.[8] Before 1963 almost all county social services boards consisted of three members. Today almost all North Carolina counties have five-member boards of social services, and only a few counties have three-member boards.

If a county has a three-member board of social services, the board of county commissioners may increase the size of the social services board from three to five members.[9] State law also allows the board of county commissioners to decrease the size of the county social services board from five to three members.[10] The commissioners' action to decrease (or increase) the size of the social services board is not subject to approval by DHHS, the state Social Services Commission, the county social services board, or the county social services director.

Members of county social services boards are appointed by the state Social Services Commission (which appoints two members of a five-member county social services board), the board of county commissioners (which appoints two members of a five-member board), and the social services board members appointed by board of county commissioners and the Social Services Commission (who appoint the remaining social services board member).[11]

The only express legal qualification for appointment to the county social services board is that the appointee be a bona fide resident of the county at the time of his or her appointment.[12]

Although state law does not require that the social services board include a county commissioner, boards of county commissioners often appoint at least one county commissioner to serve on their counties' social services boards.

County social services board members serve staggered three-year terms and generally may not serve more than two consecutive three-year terms.[13] Members of the county social services board may be removed from the board before the end of their terms only for good cause and by action of the appropriate appointing authority.[14]

State law requires the county social services board to elect one of its members as the board's chair annually at the board's July meeting.[15]

The county social services director is the board's executive officer and acts as the board's secretary.[16] The social services director, however, is not a member of the county social services board and therefore may not vote as a board member with respect to any issue coming before the board or vote to break a tie vote by the board.

Legal Status of County Social Services Boards and Board Members

Although county social services boards are established by and derive their legal status, powers, and duties from state law, they are not political subdivisions, departments, agencies, or units of state government.[17] Instead, each county social services board is a constituent part of the local government structure of each of North Carolina's one hundred counties.[18]

This does not mean, however, that the board of county commissioners has the same authority over the county social services board as it has with respect to most other county boards, commissions, or agencies. Although state law gives the board of county commissioners broad legal authority to "create, change, abolish, and consolidate offices, positions, departments, boards, commissions, and agencies of the county government," the commissioners' authority under this statute does not extend to the abolition of any county board, department, or agency—such as the county social services board— that is "established or required by [state] law."[19]

County social services boards, therefore, are local (county) government boards that are part of North Carolina's system of local (county) government but are subject to state laws that apply specifically to county social services boards and to state statutes (such as the state's Open Meetings Law) that apply generally to local (county) government boards.

Members of county social services boards are appointed public (local government) officials (not county government employees) and, as such, are subject to the provisions of North Carolina's constitution and laws governing appointed local government officials as well as the provisions of Chapter 108A of the North Carolina General Statutes that apply specifically to social services boards and board members.[20]

Notes

1. N. C. Gen. Stat. § 108A-1 (hereinafter G.S.); G.S. 153A-77. Although state law allows the creation of multicounty boards of public health and multicounty mental health authority boards, it doesn't allow the creation of multi-county boards of social services.

2. G.S. 108A-9(1).

3. G.S. 108A-9(3).

4. G.S. 108A-9(3) and (4).

5. G.S. 108A-1.

6. G.S. 108A-9(2).

7. G.S. 108A-9(5).

8. G.S. 108A-2.

9. If the county commissioners expand the social services board from three to five members, the commissioners appoint one additional social services board member for a term that expires at the same time as the term of the incumbent social services board member who was appointed by the state Social Services Commission. The state Social Services Commission appoints an additional social services board member for a term that expires at the same time as the term of the incumbent social services board member who was appointed by the board of county commissioners. The expansion of the social services board becomes effective when both of the additional social services board members have been appointed.

10. G.S. 108A-5(c). A resolution decreasing the size of the social services board from five to three members becomes effective on the first day of July following adoption of the resolution and abolishes (1) the seat held by the social services board member appointed by the state Social Services Commission for a term expiring on June 30, 2007 (or triennially thereafter) and (2) the seat held by the social services board member appointed by the board of county commissioners for a term expiring June 30, 2008 (or triennially thereafter).

11. G.S. 108A-3(b). In the case of a three-member social services board, the board of county commissioners appoints one member, the Social Services Commission appoints one member, and the two members appointed by the Social Services Commission and board of county commissioners appoint the third member. If a majority of the social services board members appointed by the Social Services Commission and the board of county commissioners cannot agree with respect to the appointment of the remaining social services board member, the authority to appoint the remaining board member is vested in the county's senior resident superior court judge. The appointment of county social services board members is discussed in more detail in Chapter 4 of this handbook.

12. *See* G.S. 108A-3(c). The qualifications for appointment to the county social services board are discussed in more detail in Chapter 4 of this handbook.

13. G.S. 108A-4, 108A-5, 108A-6. The terms of, and term limits for, county social services board members are discussed in more detail in Chapter 5 of this handbook.

14. The removal of social services board members from office is discussed in more detail in Chapter 5 of this handbook.

15. G.S. 108A-7.

16. G.S. 108A-14(a)(1).

17. *See* Meyer v. Walls, 347 N.C. 97, 489 S.E.2d 880 (1997) (holding that a county social services department is not a department, institution, or agency of the state). *Cf.* G.S. 122C-116(a) (a multicounty area mental health authority is a political subdivision of the state).

18. *See* Avery v. Burke County, 660 F.2d 111 (4th Cir. 1981); Meares v. Brunswick County, 615 F. Supp. 14 (E.D.N.C. 1985); Malloy v. Daniel, 58 N.C. App. 61, 293 S.E.2d 285 (1982). County social services boards are not "municipal or public corporations" or "bodies corporate and politic." Nor are they independent "public authorities" or "units of local government" under North Carolina's Local Government Budget and Fiscal Control

Act. *See* David M. Lawrence, *Local Government Finance in North Carolina* (Chapel Hill: Institute of Government, The University of North Carolina at Chapel Hill, 1990), 100–5.

19. G.S. 153A-76. *See also* 52 Op. N.C. Att'y Gen. 44 (1982).

20. For their service on the board, social services board members are entitled to receive a per diem payment established by the board of county commissioners and reimbursement for subsistence and travel expenses. G.S. 108A-8.

Chapter 4

Appointment of Social Services Board Members

Legal Authority to Appoint Board Members

The legal authority to appoint members of the county social services boards is vested in

- each county's board of commissioners,[1]
- the state Social Services Commission,[2] and
- a majority of the members of the county social services board who are appointed by the board of county commissioners and the Social Services Commission (or the county's senior resident superior court judge if a majority of the board members appointed by the state Social Services Commission and the board of county commissioners cannot agree on the appointment of the third social services board member).[3]

In counties with three-member boards of social services, the board of county commissioners appoints one member of the county social services board, the Social Services Commission appoints one board member, and those two board members (or the county's senior resident superior court judge) appoint the third board member.[4] In counties with five-member social services boards, the board of county commissioners and the state Social Services Commission each appoint two members of the social services board, and a majority of those four board members (or the county's senior resident superior court judge) appoints the remaining board member.[5]

Schedule for Making Appointments

Appointments to the county social services board are made on a staggered, three-year schedule that is linked to the dates on which the terms of county social services board members begin and end, as shown in table 4.1.[6]

Regular appointments (or reappointments) to the county social services board should be made shortly before the expiration of an incumbent board member's term or, if the appointing authority is unable to make the appointment before the expiration of the incumbent member's term, as soon as possible thereafter.[7]

Appointments to fill vacancies on the social services board caused by the death, resignation, or removal of a social services board member before the end of his or her term are made in the same manner as regular social services board appointments by the authority that appointed the board member who died, resigned, or was removed from the board.[8]

Qualifications for Appointment

State law establishes only one express legal qualification for appointment to the county social services board—that an appointee be a bona fide resident of the county on whose social services board he or she will serve.[9]

Although state law does not specify what it means to be a bona fide resident, bona fide residence probably is equivalent to "legal residence" or "domicile," which requires actual residence in the county and the intent to make the county one's home on a permanent, or at least indefinite, basis.[10] In determining whether a prospective appointee is a bona fide county resident, the person's statements with respect to his or her actual residence and domiciliary intent are clearly relevant but not necessarily sufficient or conclusive. Similarly, objective facts regarding a prospective appointee's residence are relevant in determining whether he or she is, in fact, a bona fide county resident, but no single fact or combination of facts regarding his or her residence is necessarily sufficient or conclusive with respect to the question. Some of the facts

Table 4.1   Social Services Board Appointment Schedule

Date Term Begins and Ends	Appointments to a Three-Member Board	Appointments to a Five-Member Board
July 1, 2007–June 30, 2010 (and triennially thereafter)	Board of County Commissioners (Board Member #1)	Board of County Commissioners (Board Member #1) Social Services Commission (Board Member #4)
July 1, 2008–June 30, 2011 (and triennially thereafter)	Social Services Commission (Board Member #2)	Social Services Commission (Board Member #2) Board of County Commissioners (Board Member #5)
July 1, 2009–June 30, 2012 (and triennially thereafter)	Social Services Board (Board Member #3)	Social Services Board (Board Member #3)

that an appointing authority might consider in determining whether an individual is a bona fide county resident include

- whether the prospective appointee actually resides in the county;
- whether he or she owns or rents a house, mobile home, or apartment as his or her personal residence in the county;
- whether the home address on his or her driver's license is located within the county;
- whether he or she is registered to vote in the county;[11] and
- how frequently, for how long, and for what purposes the appointee is absent from the county.

State law does not require a prospective appointee to be a county resident for any minimum period of time (for example, for one month or one year) before that person may be appointed to the social services board.[12] Nor does state law require that social services board appointees or members work in the county. A social services board appointee or member, therefore, may be a bona fide resident of one county even though he or she commutes to work in another county (or another state) on a daily or weekly basis.[13]

State law gives boards of county commissioners the authority to establish "qualifications for any appointive office" within county government.[14] County commissioners, therefore, may establish additional qualifications for county social services board members—including social services board members who are appointed by the state Social Services Commission, by members of the social services board, or by a resident superior court judge—as long as those additional qualifications are not inconsistent with state law.

State law does not allow county social services boards, the state Social Services Commission, or the state Department of Health and Human Services to establish additional legal qualifications for county social services board members.[15]

Each appointing authority is responsible for exercising its independent judgment and discretion in deciding whether a legally qualified individual should be appointed to the county social services board. Thus an appointing authority may, and should, consider a number of other factors, characteristics, and qualities beyond the legal qualifications required under state law when making appointments to the social services board. These additional factors, characteristics, and qualities are not, strictly speaking, additional legal qualifications for appointment to the county social services board but merely reflections of the standards, characteristics, and qualities that are desirable in persons who will serve on the social services board. For example, in determining whether an otherwise legally qualified person should be appointed to the county social services board, an appointing authority might consider whether the prospective appointee is

- motivated by a sincere and demonstrated concern for the welfare of the county's residents;
- impartial, fair, open-minded, objective, and willing to listen to other points of view;
- able to act independently, engage in creative problem-solving, and provide leadership and a sense of vision and direction for the county social services department;
- able and willing to communicate and work effectively and cooperatively with other board members, the county director of social services, the county commissioners, community groups, citizens, and state and local government agencies;
- honest and a person of unquestioned integrity;
- has any personal, family, business, or political interest that would conflict with the duties of a social services board member; and
- able and willing to devote the time and effort necessary to fulfill all responsibilities of a board member.

Legal Disqualifications

North Carolina law establishes only three express disqualifications that preclude the appointment of certain individuals to a county social services board.[16]

First, North Carolina's laws that limit multiple office-holding provide that a person is disqualified from serving on the county social services board and his or her appointment to the board is void if, at the time the appointee assumes the board position, he or she holds

- two appointive public offices or
- one elective public office and one appointive public office.[17]

Second, Section 108A-4 of the North Carolina General Statutes (hereinafter G.S.) provides that a person is not eligible to be reappointed to the county social services board if that person is an incumbent board member, has served two consecutive three-year terms on the board, and is not a county commissioner who is exempt from the two-term limit imposed by G.S. 108A-4.[18]

Third, the North Carolina Constitution disqualifies a person from holding any public office, including the office of county social services board member, if he or she has been removed from any public office by impeachment or has been found guilty of corruption or malpractice in any public office.[19]

Although the fact that a prospective appointee has been convicted of a crime may be considered in determining whether he or she should be appointed to the county social services board, the fact that a prospective appointee has been convicted of a felony does not legally disqualify him or her from being appointed to the board unless his or her citizenship rights have not been restored.[20]

The Appointment Process

State law imposes several requirements with respect to the legal process and procedures that appointing authorities must follow in making appointments to the county social services board.

When the Social Services Commission, boards of county commissioners, or county social services board members discuss prospective appointees to the social services board or appoint a person to the county social services board, they must do so during an official meeting held in accordance with the state's Open Meetings Law.[21] And the Open Meetings Law, in turn, requires

- that public notice of the meeting of the Social Services Commission, board of county commissioners, or social services board members be given;
- that the consideration of the qualifications, competence, fitness, and appointment of county social services board members by the Social Services Commission, a board of county commissioners, or county social services board members be conducted during an open session at an official, public meeting of the appointing authority; and
- that final action regarding the appointment of a county social services board member by the Social Services Commission, a board of county commissioners, or county social services board members be taken in an open session of an official, public meeting of the public body.[22]

All discussions and actions by the Social Services Commission, boards of county commissioners, and county social services boards with respect to the appointment of county social services board members, therefore, must take place in an open session of an official, public meeting of the appointing authority. Although the Open Meetings Law allows a public body to hold a closed session to discuss or take action with respect to some matters, appointments to the county social services board may not be considered or made during a closed session of a meeting of the appointing authority.[23]

In the case of appointments by the Social Services Commission and boards of county commissioners, state law requires that the appointment of a county social services board member be approved by a majority vote of the commissioners who are present at an official meeting at which a quorum is present. In the case of the Social Services Commission, state law defines a quorum as a majority of the commission's members.[24] In the case of boards of county commissioners, state law defines a quorum as a majority of a board's membership without regard to vacancies.[25]

The appointment of a county social services board member by the four (or two) social services board members appointed by the Social Services Commission and the board of county commissioners requires a unanimous vote by both of the other board members on a three-member board and a vote of at least three of the other four board members on a five-member social services board.[26] In order to vote with respect to the appointment, the other social services board members must be present at the meeting and may not vote by proxy or as absentees.[27] An incumbent social services board member who was appointed to the board by the other social services board members (or by the resident superior court judge) may not vote with respect to his or her reappointment or the selection of his or her successor (even if the other board members are deadlocked with respect to the appointment), but may participate in the board's deliberations unless prohibited from doing so under the board's policies or rules of procedure.

State law does not specify the procedure through which the senior resident superior court judge should be asked to appoint a county social services board member when a majority of the other social services board members are unable to agree with respect to the appointment. Nor does it specify the procedure by which the judge should make the appointment. It seems clear, though, that the judge is not required to hold a public hearing with respect to the appointment, to make findings of fact or explain the basis for his or her decision, or to enter a judicial order making the appointment. Once the judge makes a decision with respect to the appointment, the judge's decision is final and binding on the social services board and cannot be undone by the social services board even if all of the board members subsequently agree to appoint someone other than the person appointed by the judge.

The county social services director has no express legal authority or responsibility with respect to recruiting, nominating, or appointing members of the county social services board. State law, however, does not expressly prohibit the county social services director's providing assistance, making recommendations, or offering nominations to an appointing authority with respect to social services board appointments. If the social services director is asked or chooses to be involved in recruiting or nominating social services board members, the director's involvement should be exercised in a way that does not compromise the appointing authority's independent judgment and authority.

Except as limited by state law, each appointing authority is free to develop its own process, procedures, and policies regarding the recruitment, nomination, and appointment of social services board members.[28] At a minimum, however, an appointing authority's policies and procedures regarding the recruitment, nomination, and appointment of social services board members should

- be in writing, have been validly adopted by the appointing authority, and be publicly accessible;
- indicate the means through which potential nominees will be identified and recruited and the procedures and time frames for making and accepting nominations;

- allow sufficient time for soliciting nominations, recruiting nominees, and considering nominations;
- specify the qualifications for appointment and identify what is expected of appointees; and
- ensure that all potential appointees are qualified, are able and willing to serve if appointed, and understand the role and responsibilities of county social services board members.

Revoking or Rescinding Appointments

When an appointing authority has taken action to appoint a person to the social services board, the appointment may not be revoked or rescinded either before or after the appointee takes office.[29]

Oath of Office

As public officers, county social services board members are required to take an oath in which they swear or affirm that they will faithfully discharge the duties of their office and will support and maintain the constitutions and laws of the United States and North Carolina.[30] Failure to take the oath, however, does not affect the validity of a social services board member's appointment or the actions he or she takes as a social services board member.

Although newly appointed social services board members often take their oaths of office at the first social services board meeting following the beginning of their terms, the oath may be taken at any time between the date a member is appointed and the date he or she assumes office after the beginning of the term. The oath of office may be administered anywhere within the state by a judge, magistrate, clerk of superior court, state legislator, county or city clerk, mayor, chair of a board of county commissioners, notary public, or other specified public officials.[31] A written copy of the oath subscribed by a newly appointed social services board member must be filed with the clerk of the board of county commissioners.[32]

Notes

1. N.C. Gen. Stat. § 108A-3 (hereinafter G.S.). Each North Carolina county has an elected board of county commissioners. *See* G.S. 153A-34.

2. G.S. 108A-3. The state Social Services Commission is a thirteen-member state commission whose members are appointed by the governor for four-year terms. *See* G.S. 143B-153 and 143B-154.

3. G.S. 108A-3.

4. G.S. 108A-3(a).

5. G.S. 108A-3(b).

6. G.S. 108A-5. A "regular" appointment is any appointment other than one that is to fill the unexpired term of a board member who has resigned, died, or been removed from the board before the end of his or her term or one that is made when the size of the social services board is being increased pursuant to G.S. 108A-5.

7. When an appointing authority appoints or reappoints a person as a county social services board member, the appointing authority, the county social services director, or the county social services board should promptly notify the state Division of Social Services that the person has been appointed or reappointed and provide the division with information regarding the appointee's name, address, telephone number, and e-mail address, the date the appointee's term will expire, and the name of the public body or official that made the appointment.

8. G.S. 108A-6.

9. G.S. 108A-3(c). Read literally, the statutory requirement applies only to county social services board members who are appointed by the Social Services Commission, a board of county commissioners, or a senior resident superior court judge. The requirement does not apply to county social services board members appointed by a majority of the social services board members who were appointed by the Social Services Commission and board of county commissioners.

10. *See* Hall v. Wake County Bd. of Elections, 280 N.C. 600, 606, 187 S.E.2d 52, 55 (1972).

11. The fact that a person is registered to vote in a county creates a strong presumption that he or she is domiciled in the county, since one must be domiciled in a county in order to be registered as a voter in that county.

12. The length of a person's residence in the county, however, may be considered by the appointing authority, along with other factors (such as the length and depth of that person's involvement in the community and the breadth of his or her knowledge of the community) in determining whether the person should or should not, in the exercise of the appointing authority's judgment and discretion, be appointed to the county social services board.

13. If, however, a prospective appointee's travel or work outside the county may significantly interfere with the person's ability to perform his or her duties as a social services board member (for example, by requiring him or her to miss many social services board meetings), the appointing authority may, in the exercise of its judgment and discretion, decide that he or she should not be appointed to the social services board even though he or she is legally qualified to serve on the board.

14. G.S. 153A-25. In exercising this authority, however, the county commissioners may not waive any qualifications that are fixed by state law.

15. *See* N.C. Att'y. Gen. Advisory Op. to Dr. Sarah Morrow (July 1, 1983). A Social Services Commission rule formerly provided that county social services board members should be public-spirited citizens with demonstrated concern for the social needs of the county; that social services board members should be people who have the time to attend board meetings regularly; and that social services board members should not be selected specifically to represent any organization and should not use their membership to promote the interest of political candidates or political groups. Former 10 N.C. ADMIN. CODE 24A .0302. The rule, however, was repealed effective March 1, 1990.

16. A legal disqualification is any condition that, as a matter of constitutional, statutory, or common law, absolutely and unconditionally prohibits a person from being appointed to the county social services board or serving as a county social services board member. A legal disqualification, therefore, is different from other conditions or facts that do not legally prohibit a person from serving on the county social services board but, nonetheless, might cause an appointing authority, in the exercise of its discretion and judgment, to decide that a particular person should not be appointed to the county social services board; cause an appointing authority to take action to remove an appointee from the county social services board; preclude a county social services board member from participating in particular deliberations or decisions of the social services board; or warrant a social services board member's resignation. The removal of county social services board members is discussed in Chapter 5 of this handbook. Ethics and conflicts of interest are discussed in Chapter 6 of this handbook.

17. N.C. CONST. art. VI, § 9; G.S. 128-1.1. This prohibition does not apply to a county commissioner who is appointed to the social services board by virtue of his or her office as county commissioner. North Carolina's law limiting multiple office-holding is discussed in detail in A. Fleming Bell, II, *Ethics, Conflicts, and Offices: A Guide for Local Officials* (Chapel Hill: Institute of Government, The University of North Carolina at Chapel Hill, 1997).

18. The terms of, and term limits imposed on, county social services board members are discussed in Chapter 5 of this handbook.

19. N.C. CONST. art. VI, § 8.

20. N.C. CONST. art. VI, § 8. *See also* G.S. 13-1, which provides that a felon's citizenship rights are restored automatically upon his or her unconditional release from the state Department of Correction or under other conditions specified by law.

21. G.S. 143-318.9 through 143-318.18. The state Open Meetings Law is discussed in more detail in David M. Lawrence, *Open Meetings and Local Governments in North Carolina: Some Questions and Answers* (Chapel Hill: School of Government, The University of North Carolina at Chapel Hill, 2008). The Open Meetings Law's requirements do not apply with respect to the appointment of a county social services board member by a senior resident superior court judge.

22. G.S. 143-318.11(a)(6).

23. The Open Meetings Law also prohibits the appointment of social services board members by "secret ballot." Lawrence, *Open Meetings and Local Governments in North*

Carolina, 36. Instead each member of the appointing authority who votes with respect to the appointment of a county social services board member must do so by voice vote, show of hands, or signed ballot (and if signed ballots are used each member's vote must be publicly announced when the ballots are counted).

24. G.S. 143B-154.

25. G.S. 153A-43. State law requires all county commissioners who are present at a board meeting to vote on all matters unless they are excused by the board from voting on questions involving their own financial interest or official conduct. G.S. 153A-44. When a commissioner is not excused from voting but abstains or refuses to vote, his or her vote may be recorded as an affirmative vote, a negative vote, or a vote with the prevailing side as determined by the board's rules of procedure.

26. G.S. 108A-3. If a majority of the other social services board members are unable to agree, the appointment is made by the county's senior resident superior court judge. G.S. 108A-3.

27. 49 Op. N.C. Att'y Gen. 67 (1979). *See also* G.S. 143-318.13(a).

28. The state Social Services Commission, for example, has adopted a form for requesting that the commission appoint a nominee to a county's social services board. The commission has also adopted a rule that requires the "regional directors" employed by the state Division of Social Services to submit to the Social Services Commission the name of at least one prospective appointee who has been recommended by a local organization, interest group, or individual for appointment by the commission to a county's social services board. See 10A N.C. ADMIN. CODE 68 .0302. The rule, however, does not require the commission to appoint the individuals nominated by the regional directors, and the rule's effect has been made moot by the state's decision to eliminate the "regional director" positions in the state Division of Social Services.

29. Advisory opinion of the North Carolina Attorney General to the North Carolina Board of Public Welfare (July 29, 1966). An appointing authority, however, may remove an appointee from the social services board before the end of the appointee's term if there is good cause to do so. The removal of social services board members is discussed in Chapter 5 of this handbook.

30. N.C. CONST. art. VI, § 7; G.S. 128-5. If a county social services board member is reappointed for a second consecutive term, he or she should take a new oath of office. A county commissioner who is appointed to serve ex officio on the county social services board generally is not required to take a separate oath of office as a social services board member.

31. *See* G.S. 11-7.1.

32. G.S. 153A-26.

Chapter 5

Terms, Term Limits, and Removal of Board Members

Regular Terms

The regular term of office of all county social services board members is three years.[1]

The regular term of a county social services board member begins on July 1 if the board member is appointed and assumes office on or before July 1, or on the date an appointee assumes office, whichever is later, in accordance with the schedule set out in table 5.1.[2] The terms of all social services board members expire on June 30 in accordance with the schedule.[3]

Ex Officio Terms

When the board of county commissioners appoints a county commissioner to serve on the county's social services board, the appointment is considered (for purposes of North Carolina's multiple office-holding law) to be an ex officio appointment.[4] And when a public official holds an office in a purely ex officio capacity, his or her tenure or term in the ex officio office generally is tied to and concurrent with his or her tenure or term in the office that provided the basis for the ex officio appointment.

Table 5.1   Social Services Board Terms

Date Term Begins and Ends	Three-Member Boards	Five-Member Boards
July 1, 2007–June 30, 2010 (and triennially thereafter)	Board Member #1 (appointed by the Board of County Commissioners)	Board Member #1 (appointed by the Board of County Commissioners) Board Member #4 (appointed by the Social Services Commission)
July 1, 2008–June 30, 2011 (and triennially thereafter)	Board Member #2 (appointed by the Social Services Commission)	Board Member #2 (appointed by the Social Services Commission) Board Member #5 (appointed by the Board of County Commissioners)
July 1, 2009–June 30, 2012 (and triennially thereafter)	Board Member #3 (appointed by the other social services board members)	Board Member #3 (appointed by a majority of the other social services board members)

Some people, therefore, argue that if a county commissioner is appointed to the county social services board in an ex officio capacity, the county commissioner's tenure or term on the social services board is concurrent with his or her tenure or term on the board of county commissioners, that he or she may continue to serve on the social services board as long as he or she remains on the board of county commissioners, and that his or her tenure or term on the county social services board automatically ends as soon as he or she ceases to be a county commissioner.

It is clear, though, that this is not the case. Instead, the regular term of a county commissioner who is appointed to the county social services board by the board of county commissioners is, as is that of other county social services board members, three years and is not tied to or affected by his or her tenure or term as a county commissioner.[5]

Partial Terms

The term of a social services board member who is appointed to fill a vacancy on the social services board resulting from the death, resignation, or removal of another board member before the end of the former board member's term begins on the date he or she assumes office following his or her appointment and ends on the date that the term of his or her predecessor in office would have expired.[6] Thus the term of a social services board member who is appointed to fill a vacancy resulting from an incumbent board member's death, resignation, or removal (rather than to succeed an incumbent board member following the expiration of the incumbent's term) is not a regular three-year term but rather a partial term that is less than three years and completes the remainder of the former board member's term on the board.

Holding Over

As noted above, the terms of social services board members end June 30. If, however, an appointing authority fails to make an appointment to the social services board before the expiration of an incumbent board member's term or a newly appointed social services board member has not assumed office as of July 1, the incumbent board member continues to hold office as a social services board member after June 30 until his or her successor is appointed and assumes office.[7]

Term Limits

State law provides that a person generally may not serve more than two consecutive three-year terms on the county social services board.[8]

When a social services board member is appointed to serve the remainder of an unexpired term of a former board member, the unexpired term is not counted in applying the limit of two consecutive terms.[9]

In addition the two-consecutive-term limit does not apply to a social services board member who

1. was a county commissioner at any time during his or her first two consecutive terms on the social services board and
2. is a county commissioner at the time he or she is reappointed to the social services board.[10]

Removal of Social Services Board Members

North Carolina's social services law is silent with respect to the removal of county social services board members from office during their terms. Nonetheless, it is clear that, under general legal principles, a social services board member may be removed from office during his or her term if there is "good cause" to remove him or her from the board.

Good cause for removing a social services board member generally means a significant failure to perform the member's duties or other grounds that render the member's continuance in office contrary to the public interest. Good cause, therefore probably includes

- conviction of a felony or a crime involving moral turpitude even if the crime is unrelated to his or her official duties as a social services board member;
- bribery, corruption, extortion, or other criminal misconduct in office;
- other unlawful or grossly inappropriate conduct in office (including unlawful disclosure of confidential information);
- significant, persistent, or irreconcilable conflicts of interest;
- holding another public office that is incompatible with service on the social services board;
- misfeasance or malfeasance in office (willful or intentional neglect or failure to discharge official duties);
- neglect, inefficiency, or incompetence in performing official duties (including persistent, unexcused absences from board meetings);
- physical or mental incapacities that preclude the performance of official duties; or
- any other act or omission that brings one's public office into disrepute or that significantly and detrimentally affects a member's ability to carry out his or her official duties or that significantly and detrimentally affects the ability of the social services board, the county director of social services, or other government agencies to carry out official duties.

On the other hand, good cause does not include

- differences between a board member's political affiliation or social, economic, or political views and those of the board of county commissioners, the Social Services Commission, the other members of the social services board, or the county director of social services;

- disagreements between a board member and the board of county commissioners, the Social Services Commission, the county director of social services, or other members of the county social services board about particular social services issues; or
- problems, difficulties, or personality clashes encountered in communicating, relating, or dealing with a board member that do not unduly disrupt the board's work.

Legal authority to remove a social services board member from office is vested in the commission, board, or public officials who appointed the board member (the appointing authority). For example, a social services board member who was appointed by the Social Services Commission may be removed from office only by the Social Services Commission, and a board member appointed by the county commissioners may be removed only by the board of county commissioners.

Although state law does not clearly specify the procedure by which a social services board member may be removed from office, an appointing authority should, at a minimum, give a social services board member notice of the reasons for his or her removal from the board and an opportunity to respond to the appointing authority before the appointing authority takes final action to remove the board member from office.

The removal of a social services board member by an appointing authority is a quasi-judicial action that, on the petition of the removed board member, may be reviewed by a superior court judge through a writ of *recordari* or *certiorari*.[11] A social services board member who has been removed from office also may seek judicial review of his or her removal through a *quo warranto* proceeding (an action brought to try his or her successor's right to hold office) in superior court.[12]

Notes

1. N.C. Gen. Stat. § 108A-4 (hereinafter G.S.). A "regular" term is any term on the social services board other than the unexpired term of a social services board member who has resigned, died, or been removed from the board before the expiration of his or her term, or the term of a board member who is appointed when the size of the board is increased pursuant to G.S. 108A-5.

2. G.S. 108A-5.

3. *Id.*

4. G.S. 128-1.2. *See also* G.S. 153A-76. The term "ex officio" means "by virtue of one's office." When a person who holds a public office is appointed to another public office solely

by virtue of his or her holding the first public office, he or she is said to hold the second office ex officio. A person who holds an office ex officio does so without any warrant or appointment other than that resulting from the holding of another office and performs the duties of the ex officio office as part of the responsibilities of the office by virtue of which the ex officio appointment was made. The term ex officio does not mean that an ex officio appointee is not a voting member of the body to which he or she is appointed or has fewer or different rights than other appointees or members of the body to which he or she is appointed. Ex officio appointments are discussed in greater detail in A. Fleming Bell, II, *Ethics, Conflicts, and Offices: A Guide for Local Officials* (Chapel Hill: Institute of Government, The University of North Carolina at Chapel Hill, 1997).

5. *See* State *ex rel.* Pitts v. Williams, 260 N.C. 168, 132 S.E.2d 329 (1963); G.S. 108A-4. *See also* John L. Saxon, "Stay or Go? County Commissioners on Social Services Boards," *Popular Government* 65 (Winter 2000): 27, 30–31.

6. G.S. 108A-6.

7. *See* N.C. Const. art. VI, § 10. *See also* Baxter v. Danny Nicholson, Inc., ___ N.C. App. ___, 661 S.E.2d 892 (2008).

8. G.S. 108A-4. Terms are consecutive when a subsequent term begins immediately after the expiration of a prior term. State law does not impose a one-year or one-term waiting period with the reappointment of a former social services board member following his or her completion of two consecutive three-year terms. However, appointing authorities should not attempt to evade the purpose of the statutory term limits by appointing a person to succeed an incumbent board member with the understanding that the newly appointed board member will resign shortly thereafter, and the former board member will be reappointed to fill the remainder of the appointee's unexpired term.

9. G.S. 108A-6.

10. G.S. 108A-4.

11. G.S. 1-269; Russ v. Brunswick County Bd. of Educ., 232 N.C. 128, 59 S.E.2d 589 (1950).

12. G.S. 1-515 through 1-532; State *ex rel.* Pitts v. Williams, 260 N.C. 168, 132 S.E.2d 329 (1963).

Chapter 6

Ethical Standards for Social Services Board Members

In the context of a person's service as a county social services board member, ethics refers broadly to the standards of moral behavior that the public generally expects from persons who hold public office; to the aspirational standards for county social services board members contained in ethical codes adopted by county commissioners, county social services boards, or the North Carolina Association of County Boards of Social Services; and to the legal requirements and prohibitions that regulate the conduct and behavior of social services board members and local government officials.[1]

Ethical Expectations for Public Officials

Citizens expect all elected and appointed public officials, including county social services board members, to act ethically in their public and private lives. More specifically the public generally expects social services board members and other public officials to

- discharge the responsibilities of their office faithfully, diligently, and competently;
- comply with applicable laws governing their service as public officials;
- act in the public interest and for the public good and not use their offices for their own private benefit;
- exercise sound judgment and discretion in connection with their official duties;
- provide responsible and effective public leadership;
- act honestly, courteously, and fairly when discharging their public responsibilities; and
- maintain high standards of morality and integrity in their personal affairs.

Ethical Codes for County Social Services Board Members

Ethical codes for public officials attempt to spell out the unwritten general ethical standards with which public officials are expected to comply.[2]

Generally speaking, ethical codes for public officials may be divided into two categories: prohibitive codes and aspirational codes. A prohibitive ethical code establishes ethical standards and prescribes sanctions that may be imposed for behavior that violates those ethical standards. Aspirational codes, by contrast, specify the norms of behavior toward which public officials are expected to aspire but do not include sanctions for behavior or conduct that falls short of those standards.

Both the county social services board and the board of county commissioners have the implied legal authority to adopt aspirational ethical codes that specify the norms of behavior expected of county social services board members.

In addition the North Carolina Association of County Boards of Social Services has adopted a model code of ethics that encourages its members

- to recognize that their service on the county social services board is a community trust and that the board has a duty to the community and all of its people;
- to understand their service on the board as an expression of democratic citizenship that signifies a willingness to accept

community responsibility and the charge to preserve popular control of American public services;

- to cultivate "educated hearts" that will enable them to be sensitive to their obligations as board members;
- to provide effective and wise leadership through group thinking and action, acting as believers, planners, doers, interpreters, prophets, reformers, builders, and good citizens;
- to work to raise the ethical and professional standards of board membership;
- to become familiar with the board's role and responsibilities and the structure, programs, and organization of the county social services department;
- to devote adequate time, attention, and energy to their responsibilities as social services board members;
- to approach the board's work as a common endeavor with the belief that unity is accomplished through the resolution of differences and not in their suppression;
- to recognize the value and necessity of mutual understanding and teamwork among the board, the director, and the department's staff, and respect the different functions, roles, and responsibilities of the board, director, and staff;
- to act professionally, cooperatively, and objectively with open minds, realizing that it is not possible to lay down absolute rules for all situations, being willing to think things through with others, weighing alternatives, and exercising good judgment in choosing among them;
- to respect the dignity and worth of all people and respond to each person as an individual without distinction as to race, creed, color, or economic or social status and realize that a person's greatest possession, as well as his or her greatest contribution to society, may lie in his or her individuality and difference rather than in his or her similarity to others; and
- to maintain a community-wide perspective and know that for sound community service, the work of the social services department must be coordinated with other public and private agencies and organizations in the community.

Misconduct in Public Office

State law imposes criminal sanctions against elected or appointed public offi-cers who are found guilty of willfully failing to discharge the duties of their offices.[3]

Benefiting from Public Contracts

State law prohibits a public official, including a county social services board member, from

- attempting to influence any person involved in making or administ-ering a public contract from which the board member will receive a direct benefit[4] or
- soliciting or receiving any gift, reward, or promise of reward in exchange for recommending, influencing, or attempting to influence the award of a contract involving the county social services department.[5]

State law also generally prohibits a public official, including a county social services board member, from directly benefiting from a public contract if he or she is involved in making or administering the contract.[6]

A public official directly benefits from a public contract if he or she or a spouse has more than a 10 percent ownership or other interest in an entity that is a party to the contract, derives any income or commission directly from the contract, or acquires any property under the contract.[7] A public official is involved in making a contract if he or she participates in the development of specifications or terms or in the preparation or award of the contract or if he or she is a member of a board that takes action with respect to the contract (regardless of whether he or she participates in the action).[8] A public official is involved in administering a contract if he or she oversees the performance of the contract or has authority to make decisions regarding the contract or to interpret the contract.[9] A public official, however, is not involved in mak-ing or administering a contract solely because he or she performs ministerial duties related to the contract.[10]

Social services boards have no general legal authority to make or adminis-ter contracts involving the county social services department and, therefore, are rarely involved in making or administering public contracts.[11] As a result, the provisions of Section 14-234(a)(1) of the North Carolina General Stat-utes (hereinafter G.S.) regarding public officials who are involved in making or administering a public contract that will directly benefit them or their spouses will only rarely apply to county social services board members.

State law further provides that the provisions of G.S. 14-234(a)(1) do not apply to

- employment contracts between the county social services department and the spouse of a county social services board member if the board member does not participate in deliberating or voting with respect to the making or administering of the contract;[12]
- payments to a county social services board member or the board member's spouse for services, facilities, or supplies furnished directly to needy individuals under any federal or state social services program (for example, payments for food, prescription drugs, health care, foster care, or child care under the Food and Nutrition Services, Medicaid, foster care assistance, or subsidized child day care programs) if (1) the program is open generally to all providers of services on a nondiscriminatory basis, (2) the county social services department and its agents and employees have no control with respect to the selection of participating providers by beneficiaries of the program, (3) the payment for services is in the same amount as would be paid to any other participating provider, and (4) the board member does not participate in approving his or her payment;[13] or
- contracts with a physician, pharmacist, dentist, optometrist, veterinarian, or nurse who serves on the social services board for a county in which there is no municipality with a population of more than 15,000 according to the most recent federal census if (1) the amount of the contract does not exceed $12,500 for medical services or $25,000 for other goods or services within a twelve-month period, (2) the board member does not participate or vote with respect to the making or administering of the contract, (3) the amount of the contract is noted in the county's audited annual financial statement, and (4) the contract is noted on a list that is posted for public inspection.[14]

Violation of the conflict-of-interest provisions in G.S. 14-234 is a misdemeanor criminal offense, and contracts entered into in violation of the statute are void.[15]

The State Ethics Act

The financial disclosure requirements and ethical standards imposed on members of state government boards do not apply to county social services board members.[16]

Political Activities

Although federal and state laws limit the political activities of county social services directors and employees, these laws do not apply to county social services board members.[17]

Social services board members, however, should not use their positions on the board to promote partisan political interests or particular political candidates, parties, or platforms.[18]

Professional Responsibilities of Lawyers Who Are Board Members

Lawyers licensed in North Carolina must comply with the revised Rules of Professional Conduct (RPC) adopted by the North Carolina State Bar. These rules prohibit a lawyer who has been appointed to a county social services board from

- engaging in activities in which his or her own personal or professional interests or the interests of clients conflict with his or her duties as a public official;[19]
- appearing before the social services board on behalf of a client whom the lawyer represents;[20]
- considering any matter, participating in any decision, or attempting to influence any issue as a board member in which the lawyer, the lawyer's firm, or any client of the lawyer or the lawyer's firm has any direct or indirect interest;[21] or
- representing a client in a lawsuit against the county social services board, director, or department.[22]

The rules, however, do not prohibit

- the partner of a lawyer who serves on the county social services board from appearing before the board on behalf of a client if the lawyer who serves on the board refrains from hearing or considering the matter and does not attempt to influence, publicly or privately, the board's action;[23]

- a lawyer from appearing before the social services board while his or her spouse is serving on the board;[24] or
- a lawyer from serving on the social services board when the lawyer's partner or associate represents the social services board or department, provided that the lawyer who serves on the board refrains from participating in any deliberations or actions related to the firm's legal representation of the board or department and does not attempt to influence, publicly or privately, the board's, department's, or county's actions with respect to the firm.[25]

Nepotism

The fact that an individual's spouse, child, parent, or other close relative is employed by the county social services department does not, in and of itself, render the individual's appointment to or continued service on the county social services board unethical, improper, or unlawful. Nor does state law prohibit the county social services director from hiring a qualified person as a social services employee merely because the person is a close relative of a county social services board member.[26]

It is, however, unethical and improper for a county social services board member to use his or her position to influence the county social services director to hire, promote, or provide preferential treatment to the board member's spouse[27] or to any other person who is related to the board member by birth, adoption, or marriage.

Use and Disclosure of Confidential Information

State law allows social services board members to examine the records of persons who have applied for or are receiving public assistance or social services from the county social services department.[28]

It is unethical, improper, and unlawful, however, for a county social services board member to use or disclose information regarding persons who have applied for or are receiving public assistance and social services that is contained in county social services records or obtained by the social services department in connection with administering public assistance and social services programs for any purpose other than discharging the board's responsibilities with respect to administering public assistance and social services programs.[29]

Participation in Social Services Programs

State law expressly prohibits a county social services board member or his or her spouse from receiving payments under the State-County Special Assistance or Medicaid programs on behalf of persons who are residents or patients in adult care or nursing homes that are owned or operated, in whole or in part, by the board member or his or her spouse.[30]

County social services board members also are prohibited from being licensed as foster parents through the social services department of the county on whose social services board they serve and from being supervised or considered as a placement resource by that social services department.[31]

The fact that an individual or the individual's spouse, child, parent, sibling, or other close relative is receiving or has received public assistance or social services from the county social services department, however, does not, in and of itself, render the individual's appointment to or continued service on the county's social services board unlawful.

Conflicts of Interest

The term conflict of interest generally refers to a conflict between an individual's personal, family, business, professional, or financial interests and his or her role, responsibilities, duties, or actions as a public official.[32]

Conflicts of interest come in all shapes and sizes. They may be actual or potential. They may be real, apparent, or perceived. They may be significant or minimal. They may be continuing in nature or relate only to one particular transaction or decision. They may be avoidable or unavoidable.

Like other public officials, county social services board members are expected to act in the public interest—not for their own personal benefit—when serving as public officials. They should take reasonable actions to avoid actual and potential conflicts between their personal interests and public responsibilities and, when possible, should avoid even the appearance of acting unethically, inappropriately, or for their own benefit.

If the conflict between an individual's personal interests and his or her role as a social services board member is real, significant, and unavoidable, it may constitute good cause for requesting the board member's resignation or, if he or she fails to resign, removing him or her from the board.[33]

Notes

1. The subject of ethics in public life is discussed more fully in A. Fleming Bell, II, *Ethics, Conflicts, and Offices: A Guide for Local Officials* (Chapel Hill: Institute of Government, The University of North Carolina at Chapel Hill, 1997).

2. Ethical codes for public officials are discussed in more detail in Chapter 3 of Bell, *Ethics, Conflicts, and Offices.*

3. N.C. Gen. Stat. § 14-230 (hereinafter G.S.).

4. G.S. 14-234(a)(2).

5. G.S. 14-234(a)(3).

6. G.S. 14-234(a)(1).

7. G.S. 14-234(a1)(4).

8. G.S. 14-234(a1)(3).

9. G.S. 14-234(a1)(2).

10. G.S. 14-234(a1)(5).

11. The legal powers and duties of county social services boards with respect to public contracts are discussed in Chapter 7 and Chapter 9 of this handbook.

12. G.S. 14-234(b)(3), (b1).

13. G.S. 14-234(b)(4), (b1).

14. G.S. 14-234(d1).

15. G.S. 14-234(e), (f).

16. *See* G.S. Chapter 138A. *See also* A. Fleming Bell, II, and Norma R. Houston, "Ethics and Lobbying Reform: Applications and Implications for Local Governments," *Local Government Law Bulletin* #116 (Chapel Hill: School of Government, The University of North Carolina at Chapel Hill, 2007).

17. *See* 5 U.S.C. §§ 1501 through 1508; G.S. 126-13.

18. *See* 10 N.C. Admin. Code 24A .0302(a), (d) (repealed March 1, 1990).

19. *See* N.C. State Bar Revised Rules of Professional Conduct (RPC), Rules 6.5, 1.7(b), and 1.10.

20. N.C. State Bar Ethics Opinion CPR 177.

21. N.C. State Bar Ethics Opinion CPR 290.

22. *See* N.C. State Bar Ethics Opinion RPC 160.

23. N.C. State Bar Ethics Opinion CPR 290.

24. *Id.*

25. N.C. State Bar Ethics Opinion RPC 130.

26. A rule adopted by the state Social Services Commission prohibits county social services directors from hiring a person if he or she is the spouse, parent, sibling, child, grandparent, grandchild, stepparent, mother-in-law, father-in-law, son-in-law, daughter-in-law, brother-in-law, sister-in-law, aunt, uncle, niece, or nephew of a county social services board member. 10A N.C. Admin. Code 68 .0301. That North Carolina attorney general,

however, issued an advisory opinion on July 1, 1983, concluding that the Social Services Commission does not have the legal authority to prohibit county social services directors from hiring qualified individuals who are relatives of county social services board members.

27. *See* G.S. 14-234(a)(2).

28. G.S. 108A-11.

29. G.S. 108A-11; G.S. 108A-80.

30. G.S. 108A-47; G.S. 108A-55(d).

31. *See* 10A N.C. ADMIN. CODE 70E .1105.

32. Conflicts between the private interests of public officials and their public responsibilities are discussed in more detail in Chapter 4 and Chapter 5 of Bell, *Ethics, Conflicts, and Offices.*

33. The removal of county social services board members is discussed in Chapter 5 of this handbook.

Chapter 7

The Board's Legal Authority, Powers, and Duties

Sources of the Board's Legal Authority

State law defines the nature and extent of the county social services board's legal authority, powers, and duties and the limits on the board's legal authority, powers, and duties.[1]

Many of the powers and duties of county social services boards are specified in Chapter 108A (Social Services) of the North Carolina General Statutes (hereinafter G.S.). State law, however, also expressly provides that the state Social Services Commission, the state Department of Health and Human Services (DHHS), or the board of county commissioners may assign additional duties and responsibilities to county social services boards.[2] Neither the Social Services Commission, DHHS, nor a board of county commissioners, however, may limit the legal authority of a county social services board or assign the social services board's powers, duties, or functions to another public official, board, or agency if state law allows or requires the county social services board to exercise the authority, power, duty, or function in question.[3]

In addition to the legal powers that are expressly granted by state law, a county social services board is authorized to exercise any power that

- is reasonably necessary to enable it to exercise the powers that are expressly granted to it under state law;

- is reasonably implied by, or incident to, the powers expressly granted to it under state law; or
- is essential to the accomplishment of the board's purpose.

For example, a county social services board has the implied legal authority to evaluate the job performance of the county social services director because evaluation of the director's performance is necessary to enable the board to discharge its responsibilities to determine the director's salary, consult with the director about problems affecting the director or the county social services department, and take disciplinary action against the director if his or her job performance is unsatisfactory.

Nature and Scope of the Board's Authority

In some instances the social services board's authority with respect to a particular matter is exclusive. The county social services board, for example, has the exclusive power to dismiss the county social services director but must do so in accordance with the requirements and limitations of the State Personnel Act.[4]

In other instances the board's power is shared and must be exercised jointly with another public official, board, or agency. The social services board's decision regarding the social services director's salary, for example, must be approved by the board of county commissioners.[5]

When state law authorizes, but does not require, a county social services board to exercise a specific power, the board generally has the discretion to exercise its authority or to refrain from exercising its authority and, unless prohibited by law, may delegate its legal authority to another public official, board, or agency. In some instances, state statutes or rules expressly authorize the county social services board to delegate a particular responsibility to the county social services director.[6]

County social services boards are prohibited from exercising powers that are not granted to them, either explicitly or implicitly, by state law or that are vested by state law in another public official, board, or agency. A county social services board, for example, has no authority to hire or fire employees of the county social services department (other than the county social services director) because state law [G.S. 108A-14(a)(2)] vests that authority in the county social services director rather than the social services board.

When exercising their legal powers and duties, county social services boards are required to comply with applicable provisions of federal and state law (for example, the requirements of the state Open Meetings Law, the State Personnel Act, and federal and state statutes prohibiting discrimination in employment).

The Board's Legal Duties and Responsibilities

State law requires the county social services board to discharge the following legal duties and responsibilities:[7]

1. appoint the county social services director in accordance with the rules and procedures established by the State Personnel Act and the State Personnel Commission;[8]
2. determine, with the approval of the board of county commissioners, the social services director's salary;[9]
3. consult with and advise the social services director about problems involving the county social services department;[10]
4. assist the county social services director in planning the social services department's proposed budget;[11]
5. transmit or present the proposed social services budget to the board of county commissioners;[12]
6. advise county and municipal authorities with respect to developing policies and plans to improve the community's social conditions.[13]
7. establish county policies for social services programs that are consistent with applicable federal and state laws, rules, and policies;[14]
8. appoint the third member of the county social services board;[15]
9. elect the board's chair;[16]
10. meet at least once per month or more often if a meeting is called by the board chair;[17] and
11. carry out other duties and responsibilities assigned to the board by the North Carolina General Assembly, the Social Services Commission, the DHHS, or the board of county commissioners.[18]

Additional Legal Powers and Authority

State law also authorizes the county social services board to perform the following functions and exercise the following legal powers:[19]

1. discipline or dismiss the county social services director in accordance with the rules and procedures established by the State Personnel Act and the State Personnel Commission;[20]
2. evaluate the social services director's performance;
3. adopt rules of procedure for board meetings;
4. remove the third member of the social services board for "good cause" during his or her term;[21]
5. approve the board of county commissioners' appointment of the county attorney or a licensed attorney to serve as a special county attorney for social services matters;[22]
6. decide, in standard Work First counties and in accordance with state rules, whether a family may receive Work First Family Assistance payments for more than twenty-four months (cumulative) and, if so, the length of time the family may continue to receive assistance (subject to state and federal limitations);[23]
7. approve or disapprove all applications for State-County Special Assistance (financial assistance for elderly or disabled residents of adult care homes);[24]
8. determine whether there is sufficient evidence that a person who has applied for or received State-County Special Assistance has committed fraud and, if so, what action the social services department should take with respect to such fraud;[25]
9. approve or disapprove all applications for Medicaid;[26]
10. determine whether there will be a local waiting list policy for social services funded under the Social Services Block Grant (SSBG) and, if so, adopt such a policy;[27]
11. decide whether the county social services department will use the declaration method of eligibility determination rather than the verification method for SSBG-funded social services for which eligibility is based on family income;[28]
12. determine, in the absence of a local transportation development plan, the transportation services that the county social services department will provide to clients who receive certain services funded under the SSBG;[29] and
13. approve all contracts under which the county social services department voluntarily provides services to or for another governmental or private agency or any person in exchange for a fee covering the cost

of the services and approve, with the board of county commissioners, the fee plan recommended by the county social services director.[30]

County social services boards, however, do not have the legal authority, power, or duty

1. to hire, supervise, promote, discipline, or fire employees of the county social services department other than the director;
2. to establish personnel policies for county social services employees;
3. to determine the salary schedule and employment benefits for county social services employees;
4. to approve or administer the county social services department's budget; or
5. to approve or execute contracts involving the county social services department.

Notes

1. Because a county social services board's authority, powers, duties, and responsibilities are based on state law, the North Carolina General Assembly may enact legislation to increase, change, or decrease the authority, powers, duties, or responsibilities of social services boards.

2. N.C. GEN. STAT. § 108A-9(5) (hereinafter G.S.). When the Social Services Commission or state Department of Health and Human Services assigns additional duties and responsibilities to county social services boards, these additional duties and responsibilities may be specified in administrative rules (codified in the North Carolina Administrative Code) or other statements of policy or procedure. When the board of county commissioners assigns additional duties or responsibilities to the county social services board, these additional duties or responsibilities should be specified in a resolution or ordinance adopted by the board of county commissioners.

3. See G.S. 153A-76 (limiting the county commissioners' authority to discontinue or reassign powers, duties, or functions of a local government board if those powers, duties, or functions have been assigned to the board by state law).

4. G.S. 108A-12(a).

5. G.S. 108A-13.

6. See G.S. 108A-43(a); 10A N.C. ADMIN. CODE 21B .0205(b); 10A N.C. ADMIN. CODE 71P .0508(e).

7. Some of these duties are discussed in more detail in Chapter 8 and Chapter 9 of this handbook.

8. G.S. 108A-9(1); G.S. 108A-12(a).

9. G.S. 108A-13.

10. G.S. 108A-9(3).

11. *Id.*

12. G.S. 108A-9(4).

13. G.S. 108A-9(2).

14. G.S. 108A-1.

15. G.S. 108A-3(a), (b). Strictly speaking, this authority is exercised by a majority of the four (or two) social services board members who have been appointed by the board of county commissioners and the Social Services Commission, rather than by the board as a whole.

16. G.S. 108A-7.

17. *Id.*

18. G.S. 108A-9(5).

19. Some of these powers are discussed in more detail in Chapter 8 and Chapter 9 of this handbook.

20. G.S. 108A-12(a).

21. Strictly speaking, this power is exercised by a majority of the four (or two) social services board members who have been appointed by the board of county commissioners and the Social Services Commission rather than by the board as a whole.

22. G.S. 108A-16.

23. The board may delegate this authority to the county social services director.

24. G.S. 108A-43(a). The board may delegate this authority to the county social services director.

25. 10A N.C. Admin. Code 71P .0508(e).

26. 10A N.C. Admin. Code 21B .0205(b).

27. 10A N.C. Admin. Code 71R .0803(b)(1).

28. 10A N.C. Admin. Code 71R .0701.

29. 10A N.C. Admin. Code 71I .0101.

30. G.S. 108A-10.

Chapter 8

The Board's Responsibilities Regarding the Social Services Director and Employees

Appointing the Social Services Director

The county social services board has the exclusive authority to appoint the county social services director.[1] In appointing the director, however, the board must comply with the requirements set forth in the State Personnel Act and rules adopted by the State Personnel Commission and do so in accordance with the procedures required under the state Open Meetings Law.[2]

Deciding who should be appointed as the county's social services director is one of the most important decisions that a social services board may be called upon to make. A county social services board, therefore, should devote the time, attention, and effort necessary to develop and implement a hiring process that both ensures the board will select and retain the best-qualified person to serve as the director and will reduce the likelihood of legal challenges by unsuccessful applicants.

There are at least five major steps that a social services board should follow when it appoints a new social services director.[3]

The first step is to determine the characteristics, experience, and skills that the board feels a new social services director should have in order to successfully and effectively manage and lead the county social services department.[4]

To do this the board should first discuss and make a list of the potential issues, challenges, and demands that a new social services director will face. Then, considering the potential issues, challenges, and demands, the board should develop a list of the characteristics, experience, knowledge, skills, and abilities that it feels a new social services director should have in order to respond effectively to the issues, challenges, or demands. Finally, the board should identify which of the desired characteristics, experience, and skills are most important and develop a profile of its "ideal" candidate, which will be used to write an advertisement for the position and provide objective criteria to screen applicants, interview candidates, and select the most qualified candidate.[5]

The second step is to plan a hiring strategy and, if necessary, appoint an acting or interim social services director. In doing so, the board should remember that the time it spends in carefully planning the hiring process will often save time in the long run by making the process more efficient and avoiding delays and disagreements.

The board's hiring strategy should

- outline the tasks that must be completed to recruit and appoint a new social services director,
- identify who will be responsible for each task, and
- establish a timetable for the completion of each task.[6]

Among other things, the board's strategy should address

- whether the board will consider inside candidates for the position,
- how the position will be advertised,
- who will screen applications for the position,
- how candidates will be interviewed,
- how references will be checked,
- how the board will select its final candidate, and
- the minimum and maximum salary that can be offered.

As part of its hiring strategy, the board should consult with and request assistance from the county's personnel or human resources office or the local government staff of the Office of State Personnel to assist the board in the process of recruiting and screening applicants, interviewing candidates, selecting the most suitable candidate, and appointing a new director and to ensure that the board complies with applicable requirements of federal and state law.[7]

If the director's position is vacant and the board is unable to appoint a new director immediately, the board should appoint an acting or interim social services director to serve until it appoints a new director.[8] (An incumbent county social services board member may not serve as the acting or interim director of social services.) An emergency appointment as acting social services director generally may not exceed sixty work days.[9] A temporary appointment as acting or interim social services director generally may not exceed twelve months.

The third step is to advertise the position and screen applications.

If the board decides to fill the director's position through recruitment within the county social services department and has not adopted an "understudy" arrangement in which a particular social services employee has been designated as the director's potential successor, state rules require the board to post a job vacancy announcement for the position in a prominent location at the county social services department.[10] If the board decides to fill the director's position through open recruitment (that is, by considering applicants other than current employees of the county social services department), the board must list the position with the local Employment Security Commission office and establish an application period of at least seven days. At a minimum, the job vacancy notice must describe the director's position, the minimum qualifications for the position, and the procedures to apply for the position.[11]

Applications for the director's position should be submitted to the board or its designee and screened by the board, a subcommittee of the board, or the board's designee to ensure that they are complete and meet the minimum requirements established by the board and state rules.[12] State rules generally require that a person who is appointed as a county social services director have

- a master's degree in social work and two years of supervisory experience in the delivery of client services;[13]
- a thorough knowledge of the legal and philosophical basis for public welfare programs;
- considerable knowledge of principles and practice of social work;
- a thorough knowledge of management principles, techniques, and practices;
- knowledge of the agency's organization, operation and objectives and applicable federal and state laws, rules, and regulations;

- the ability to exercise sound judgment in analyzing situations and making decisions;
- the ability to direct employees and programs in the various areas of responsibility; and
- the ability to develop and maintain effective working relationships with the general public and with federal, state, and local officials.[14]

The board, a subcommittee of the board, or the board's designee should then identify the applicants who appear to most closely match the board's profile of its ideal candidate, determine which of those applicants will be considered as candidates for the director's position, and schedule an interview with each candidate.[15]

The fourth step in the process of appointing a new social services director is for the board to interview each candidate and to assess and compare the relative strengths, weaknesses, qualifications, and suitability of each candidate.

When the board interviews a candidate for the director's position or discusses the qualifications or suitability of candidates, it must do so at an official board meeting in accordance with the requirements established by the state Open Meetings Law.[16] Although the board must give public notice of a meeting at which the board will interview candidates for the director's position or discuss the qualifications or suitability of candidates, the interview and discussion should be done in a closed session of the meeting pursuant to Section 143-318.11(a)(6) of the North Carolina General Statutes (hereinafter G.S.). All board members should participate in interviewing every candidate so they can all hear each candidate's responses and won't have to rely on information filtered through another member's perspective when they assess and compare the candidates.

The board's interview process should be structured in such a way that it will allow members to make reliable judgments about the qualifications, skills, and characteristics that the board has determined a new social services director should have and to make valid comparisons among the candidates for the director's position.[17] Questions asked of candidates should focus on the skills, characteristics, and qualifications required for the position, their motivation and desire to serve as the county's social services director, and how they might respond to some of the issues, problems, and challenges they might confront as the new director. Board members should avoid asking questions about irrelevant and inappropriate matters, including the race, ethnicity, marital status, or religious beliefs of a candidate.[18] A structured interview process, developed with the assistance of a qualified human resources professional, allows the board to make valid comparisons among candidates and treat each candidate fairly by asking each one the same set of questions. In addition, boards should consider developing and using a rating instrument that allows board members to evaluate each area of a candidate's knowledge, experience, and skills using a uniform scale.

Board members and others involved in interviewing candidates or assessing the qualifications and suitability of candidates must protect the confidentiality of information regarding applicants for the director's position.[19]

The fifth step in appointing a new social services director is for the board to select a final candidate, check the candidate's employment references, educational qualifications, criminal history, and eligibility for employment as a U.S. citizen or immigrant, negotiate the proposed salary and other conditions of employment, and make the appointment.

The board's selection and appointment of a new social services director must be based upon a relative consideration of the qualifications of the applicants for the position.[20] Advantage must be given to those applicants determined to be best qualified, and the board must document its decision to verify that this advantage was granted and explain the basis for its decision.[21] A social services board, however, also must give preference to applicants who served honorably in the armed services during designated periods of war, to applicants who are veterans of the armed forces and who suffered disabling service-related injuries during peacetime, and to spouses or surviving spouses of certain military veterans.[22]

Although the county social services board may discuss the qualifications of applicants for the director's position during closed session, the board's decision to appoint an individual as the county social services director must be made by majority vote of a quorum of the board members present at an open session of an official board meeting.[23]

The board's appointment of a county social services director is not subject to the approval of the board of county commissioners, the state Department of Health and Human Services, or any other public agency or official.[24]

When an individual is appointed as a new county social services director, he or she must serve a probationary appointment of three to nine months.[25]

Determining the Director's Salary

State law provides that the salary of the county social services director is determined by the county social services board with the approval of the board of county commissioners.[26]

The director's salary, however, must fall within the county's state-approved salary plan and schedule for county social services employees, which must establish a minimum salary that is at least 20 percent and not more than 60 percent more than the minimum salary for the highest position (other than deputy director or attorney) supervised by the director.[27]

Supervising, Advising, and Evaluating the Director

The county social services director is directly accountable to the county social services board. And the board, in turn, is responsible for providing general supervision of the director and general oversight of the county social services department.

State law, therefore, expressly requires the board to advise or "consult with" the director about "problems" relating to the director's office or the county social services department.[28] The board, however, does not have the authority to overrule the director's decisions or interfere with the director's management of the department when state law vests authority for the department's management or administration in the director.

Although state law does not require the social services board to evaluate the social services director, the board has the implied authority and responsibility to do so. And because state law does not address the procedure for evaluating the county social services director, each county social services board has the legal authority to adopt its own policies and procedures for evaluating the director, including

- the frequency and timing of evaluations,
- the criteria and standards against which the director will be evaluated, and
- the process for conducting evaluations.[29]

Regular and thorough evaluations of the social services director by the board are important because they provide necessary feedback to the director about whether he or she is meeting the board's expectations and allow the board to review the director's work objectively and systematically rather than in response to some immediate crisis or problem.

Some boards, however, are reluctant to evaluate the agency's director. Some board members find it difficult to talk openly and honestly about the positive and negative aspects of the director's performance. And others believe that there is no need to formally evaluate the director's work when everything appears to be going well.

Even when a board agrees that evaluating the director's performance is both necessary and desirable, the board may encounter a number of problems in evaluating the director. For example, the board may

- be unclear or disagree about the purpose of the evaluation;
- devote insufficient time to planning the evaluation process or conducting the evaluation;
- use an evaluation form or process that has been developed by another public agency or official but is not well suited for the board's use;
- disagree with respect to the procedures that will be used for the evaluation; or
- disagree about which criteria the board will use to evaluate the director or whether the director has met the board's criteria or expectations.

Social services boards, therefore, should develop policies and procedures that address

- the purposes of the board's evaluation of the director,
- the frequency and timing of evaluations,
- the board's expectations of the director,
- the standards and methods for evaluating the director,
- the forms the board will use to evaluate the director, and
- the process by which the board will evaluate the director.

If a newly appointed director is serving a probationary period of employment, the board should evaluate the director before the end of the period to decide whether the director should be retained in the position after the probationary period. After a social services director has completed the probationary period, the board should evaluate the director on an annual basis.

In developing the evaluation process and evaluating the director, social services boards should seek and consider the director's input. One purpose of an evaluation is to provide the director with useful feedback regarding his or her future work and professional development. Involving the director in the evaluation process gives the director an opportunity to tell the board what he or she would like to learn from the evaluation process. In addition boards should consider the director's assessment of his or her work, strengths, and weaknesses as well as the board's perspective by asking the director to do a self-evaluation as part of the process.

If the board decides to seek information from others to evaluate the director's performance, the board should not accept information on the condition that the source and substance of the information will not be revealed to the director.[30]

Most social services boards that evaluate social services directors ask each board member to evaluate the director using the standards and methods specified by the board and then meet to discuss the evaluations completed by each member. The board's discussion of the director's performance must take place at an official board meeting but be conducted during a closed session called pursuant to G.S. 143-318.11(a)(6). Each board member should be given time to express his or her judgment regarding the director's performance with respect to each standard. The board should then discuss any differences among the members' evaluations, consider any additional information or input from the social services director or other sources that might help the board make an informed decision, and, if possible, agree on a single rating by the board with respect to each of the criteria or areas covered by the evaluation.

After the board has completed its evaluation, the board should

- provide a copy of its final evaluation to the director,
- discuss the final evaluation with the director,
- note any areas of the director's performance that are unsatisfactory or need improvement,
- agree with the director on any particular actions the board feels the director should take to improve his or her performance and the time during which these actions should be completed,
- discuss and revise if necessary the board's expectations for the director's performance in the coming year,
- ask the director to develop goals or a work plan for the coming year, and
- assess (and revise if necessary) the evaluation process used by the board.

All information related to the board's evaluation of the director is part of the director's personnel record and is protected by the confidentiality requirements of state law.[31]

Disciplining or Dismissing the Director

The county social services board has the exclusive legal authority to discipline or dismiss (fire) the county social services director.[32] The board, however, must exercise its authority in accordance with the applicable provisions of the State Personnel Act (SPA) and the rules adopted by the State Personnel Commission (SPC).

Under the SPA and the SPC rules, a social services board's ability to dismiss a social services director depends, in part, on whether the director is a "career" employee. A county social services director has attained career status if he or she has successfully completed his or her initial probationary period as director and has been continuously employed by a state or county agency subject to the SPA for a period of at least twenty-four months immediately prior to being disciplined or dismissed.[33]

A county social services director who has attained career status may be dismissed by the county social services board only

- for unsatisfactory job performance or unacceptable personal conduct and
- in accordance with the procedures established by or pursuant to the SPA.[34]

Unsatisfactory job performance is defined as "work-related performance that fails to satisfactorily meet job requirements as specified in the [employee's] job description, work plan or as directed by the [employee's supervisor or agency management]."[35] Examples of unsatisfactory job performance include failure to produce accurate work, failure to produce a sufficient quantity of work, failure to produce work of acceptable quality, failure to produce work in a timely manner, and failure to attend work on a regular basis (e.g., abuse of leave, tardiness, and absenteeism).

Unsatisfactory job performance that results in the creation of the potential for death or serious harm to a client, an employee, a member of the general public, or a person over whom the director has responsibility or that results in the loss of or damage to agency property or funds that causes a serious impact on the agency constitutes grossly inefficient job performance.[36]

Unacceptable personal conduct is defined as (1) intentional or unintentional work-related or non–work-related conduct for which no reasonable employee should expect to receive a prior warning; (2) work-related conduct that violates federal or state law; (3) conviction of a felony or criminal offense involving moral turpitude that is detrimental to or impacts a director's service to the agency; (4) willful violation of known or written work rules; (5) conduct unbecoming a public official or employee that is detrimental to the agency; (6) abuse of a client, patient, student, or other person for whom the director has charge or responsibility; (7) falsification of an employment application or other employment documentation; (8) willful failure or refusal to carry out a reasonable order from an authorized supervisor; or (9) absence from work after all authorized leave credits and benefits have been exhausted.[37]

If a county social services board believes that there may be good reason to consider disciplining or dismissing the director due to allegedly unsatisfactory job performance or unacceptable personal conduct, the board should immediately request advice and assistance from the county's human resources office or the Office of State Personnel's local government team.

If the board determines that the director's job performance is unsatisfactory or that the director's personal conduct is unacceptable and the issue regarding the director's performance or conduct has not been satisfactorily resolved, the board may, subject to the limitations imposed by the SPA and SPC rules discussed below,

- decide not to take formal disciplinary action,[38]
- give the director a written warning,
- suspend the director for a period of at least five work days and not more than ten work days without pay,
- reduce the director's salary, or
- dismiss (fire) the director.[39]

All discussions by the board regarding the director's performance, competence, fitness, or character or to hear or investigate any complaint, charge, or grievance by or against the director must take place at an official board meeting and during a closed session pursuant to G.S. 143-318.11(a)(6).[40] If, however, the board determines that the director should be dismissed, final action to dismiss the director must be taken by the board in an open meeting and not during a closed session.[41]

If the board decides to issue a warning to the director based on unsatisfactory job performance or unacceptable personal conduct, the warning must

- be given to the director in writing;
- inform the director that it is a written disciplinary warning and not some other nondisciplinary process such as counseling;
- inform the director of the specific incident of unsatisfactory job performance or unacceptable personal conduct that is the basis for the warning;
- inform the director what specific actions, changes, or improvements, if any, must be taken to correct or address the unsatisfactory job performance or unacceptable personal conduct;
- advise the director of the time frame within which he or she must take corrective action;[42]
- advise the director of the consequences of failing to take the required corrective action; and
- advise the director of his or her right, if any, to contest or appeal the warning.[43]

The board may discipline the director for unsatisfactory job performance or unacceptable personal conduct by suspending the director without pay for a period of at least five work days and not more than ten work days or by reducing (with the concurrence of the board of county commissioners and within the range allowed by the applicable salary schedule for the director's salary) the director's salary.[44] A social services board may suspend the director without pay or reduce the director's salary based on the director's unacceptable personal conduct or grossly inefficient job performance regardless of whether the director has received a prior written warning or other disciplinary action for unacceptable personal conduct or unsatisfactory job performance. A social services director, however, may not be suspended without pay or have his or her salary reduced based on his or her unsatisfactory job performance (other than grossly inefficient job performance) unless he or she has received at least one prior written warning or other disciplinary action that is still "active."[45]

A county social services board may dismiss the social services director for unacceptable personal conduct or for grossly inefficient job performance without having taken prior disciplinary action against the director with respect to the director's performance or conduct and without having given the director prior warning regarding the conduct that is the basis for the board's action.[46] By contrast, the board may not dismiss the social services director for unsatisfactory job performance (other than grossly inefficient job performance) unless there are at least two "active" written warnings or disciplinary actions involving the director's performance or conduct.[47]

Before taking action to dismiss a director (or to suspend the director or reduce the director's salary) for unsatisfactory job performance or unacceptable personal conduct, the board must conduct a pre-disciplinary conference.[48] The purpose of the pre-disciplinary conference is to ensure that severe disciplinary action is warranted and is not based on misinformation or mistake.[49] The director must be given oral or written notice of the conference and the basis for the possible dismissal, suspension, or reduction in salary.[50] At the conference, the board must give the director written notice of the specific reasons that the board is considering as the basis for possible dismissal, suspension, or demotion and a summary of the information that might support his or her dismissal, suspension, or demotion.[51] The board must give the director an opportunity to respond and to offer information or arguments in support of the director's position.[52] No witnesses or attorneys, however, may attend the conference, and neither the board nor the director may tape record the conference.[53] If the director fails to attend the pre-disciplinary conference, the board may proceed without the director's input.

After the pre-disciplinary conference, the board must make a decision regarding the director's dismissal, suspension, or demotion. If the board decides to dismiss the director, it must take action to do so during an open meeting. The board must notify the director in writing of the board's decision to dismiss, suspend, or demote the director within a reasonable time but not earlier than the start of the first business day following the board's decision. The notice must be delivered to the director in person or by certified mail, inform the director of the disciplinary action that is being taken, state the reasons for the board's action and the effective date of the action, and inform the director of his or her right to appeal the board's action.[54]

A career county social services director who is dismissed, suspended, or demoted for unsatisfactory job performance or unacceptable personal conduct has the right to appeal his or her dismissal, suspension, or demotion.[55]

Except in cases involving allegations of discrimination in connection with a disciplinary action, a social services director who is dismissed, suspended, or demoted must appeal the board's decision in accordance with any applicable county personnel ordinance or grievance policy within fifteen days of his or her receipt of written notice of the board's action.[56]

If the board refuses to change its decision as a result of the director's grievance, the director may appeal the board's decision by commencing a contested case pursuant to North Carolina's Administrative Procedure Act.[57] To do so, the director must file a petition with the North Carolina Office of Administrative Hearings (OAH) within thirty days of receipt of the board decision and serve a copy of the petition on the board.[58]

If the director files a petition with OAH, OAH will assign an administrative law judge (ALJ) to hear the case.[59] The director and board will be given at least fifteen days' notice of the hearing.[60] At the hearing, both the board and the director have the right to be represented by legal counsel, to call, examine, and cross-examine witnesses, to present evidence, and to make legal arguments to the ALJ.[61] If the director alleges that he or she was suspended or dismissed without just cause, the board has the burden of proving, by a preponderance of the evidence, that it had just cause to suspend or dismiss the director.[62]

After the hearing, the ALJ is required to issue a recommended decision to the State Personnel Commission and send a copy of the recommended decision to the board and director.[63] Under state law, the State Personnel Commission must adopt the ALJ's recommended decision as the commission's decision in the case unless it determines that the ALJ's decision is clearly contrary to the preponderance of admissible evidence in the record of the hearing or erroneous as a matter of law.[64] A copy of the commission's decision must be served personally or by certified mail on the director, the board, the county (if the county has intervened), the parties' attorneys, and OAH.[65]

If the commission determines that the social services board unlawfully discriminated against the director on the basis of his or her race, religion, color, creed, national origin, sex, age, or handicapping condition, the commission will issue a final agency decision that requires the board to reinstate the director and pay the director the salary he or she would have received but for the board's action.[66]

In cases in which the commission does not find evidence of unlawful discrimination but determines that the board did not follow the proper legal procedures in suspending or dismissing the director, did not have just cause to suspend or dismiss the director, or acted arbitrarily or capriciously in suspending or dismissing the director, the commission will issue an advisory decision to the board recommending that the director's suspension or dismissal be set aside.[67] In these cases, the social services board must issue a written final decision that accepts, rejects, or modifies the commission's advisory decision within ninety days and serve the final decision on the director, the director's attorney, and the county (if the county intervened in the administrative proceeding).[68] If the board rejects or modifies the commission's advisory decision, it must state its reasons for doing so.[69]

After the social services board or the SPC issues a final decision, the director may seek judicial review of the decision by filing a petition in the superior court pursuant to Article 4 of the state Administrative Procedure Act.[70] A petition for judicial review must be filed within thirty days of service of the board's or commission's final decision and served on the county social services board.[71]

If the director seeks judicial review, the superior court judge must reverse or remand the board decision if the court determines that the board heard new evidence after receiving the advisory decision or did not accept the advisory decision and failed to specify the reasons for rejecting it.[72] If the board's final decision does not adopt the commission's recommended decision, the superior court judge is not bound by the board's findings of fact or conclusions of law and may grant relief to the director if the judge determines, based on his or her de novo review of the record of the administrative hearing, that the board's decision was unlawful.[73] If the board's decision adopts the commission's recommended decision, the judge may reverse the board's decision if, using the "whole record" test for judicial review, the board's findings of fact are unsupported by substantial, admissible evidence in the record.[74] The superior court judge also may reverse the board's decision if the judge determines that the decision was unconstitutional, exceeded the board's statutory authority, was made upon unlawful procedure, was legally erroneous, or was arbitrary, capricious, or an abuse of discretion.[75]

If the superior court judge affirms the board's decision, the director may appeal the superior court decision to the North Carolina Court of Appeals.[76]

State law also gives county social services directors the right to file grievances and appeals regarding certain employment practices that do not involve disciplinary suspensions or dismissals, including but not limited to

- workplace harassment based on age, sex, race, color, national origin, religion, creed, or handicapping condition;

- denials of training due to age, sex, race, color, national origin, religion, creed, political affiliation, or handicapping condition; and
- violations of the federal Fair Labor Standards Act, the federal Age Discrimination in Employment Act, the federal Family Medical Leave Act, and the federal Americans with Disabilities Act.[77]

The Board's Authority Regarding Social Services Employees

County social services boards have no legal authority to

- hire, evaluate, supervise, promote, or fire county social services employees other than the county social services director;
- determine the minimum qualifications or salaries of county social services employees; or
- adopt personnel rules and policies governing county social services employees.[78]

In counties with a county manager, the manager is responsible for hiring and firing most county employees.[79] This is not true, however, with respect to employees of the county social services department. Instead, state law gives the county social services director the exclusive authority to hire, supervise, and discipline county social services employees.[80]

Social services boards, therefore, have no authority to hire, evaluate, supervise, manage, promote, discipline, or fire any employee of the county social services department other than the social services director or to approve or disapprove the director's decisions regarding the hiring, evaluation, promotion, discipline, or firing of a county social services employee.[81] They should refrain from any action that might impinge upon the director's authority to hire, supervise, or discipline social services employees.

Unlike most county employees, county social services employees and the positions they hold are subject to the provisions of the State Personnel Act.[82] This means that county social services employees must be hired in accordance with the merit selection rules and procedures and position classification plan established by the State Personnel Commission, that they must meet the minimum education, experience, and training qualifications established by the State Personnel Commission, and once they have obtained career status, they may be dismissed only for unacceptable personal conduct or unsatisfactory job performance in accordance with the procedures established by the State Personnel Act and rules adopted by the State Personnel Commission.[83]

State law, however, also authorizes the board of county commissioners to establish a salary plan or schedule for all county employees and provides that, if the board does so and files the county's salary plan or schedule with the State Personnel Director, the county's salary plan or schedule, rather than the salary plan or schedule adopted under the State Personnel Act, will apply to county social services employees in the same manner as they do to other county employees.[84] In addition, the board of county commissioners effectively determines the number of county social services employees through its approval of the social services budget.

State law also allows the board of county commissioners to adopt ordinances, rules, or policies or provide for the adoption of policies and rules that govern the work schedules and holidays for county employees, service award and incentive award programs for county employees, working conditions of county employees, and other personnel matters regarding county employees.[85] This also applies to county social services employees unless the county rules are inconsistent with the provisions of the State Personnel Act or rules adopted by the State Personnel Commission that govern county social services employees.

By contrast, state law does not give the county social services board any authority to approve the salary plan or schedule for county social services employees or to adopt personnel rules or policies for county social services employees.

This doesn't mean, though, that county social services boards shouldn't be concerned with the size of the county social services staff or the salaries, benefits, working conditions, training, qualifications, and morale of county social services employees. Indeed, the social services board should encourage and support the social services director in his or her efforts to ensure that the county department of social services has sufficient staff to adequately perform its work, that the salaries, benefits, and working conditions of county social services employees are such that the department can hire and retain qualified employees, and that county social services employees receive the training they need to do their work.

The Board's Authority Regarding the Social Services Attorney

Social services boards generally have no authority to appoint, retain, or hire an attorney to provide legal services to the county social services department.[86]

Two exceptions to this general rule may arise, however, if the board of county commissioners

- authorizes the social services board to retain an attorney to provide legal services to the county social services department; or
- decides to appoint the county attorney or another attorney as the "special county attorney for social services" under the provisions of G.S. 108A-16.

Notes

1. N.C. Gen. Stat. § 108A-9(1) (hereinafter G.S.); G.S. 108A-12. A county social services board may not appoint a new county social services director unless the incumbent director has died or resigned, is retiring, or has been dismissed.

2. See G.S. 126-3; G.S. 126-4; G.S. 126-5(a)(2); 25 N.C. Admin. Code 01I .1901 through 01I .1905. The state Open Meetings Law is discussed in Chapter 10 of this handbook.

3. See Kurt Jenne and Margaret Henderson, "Hiring a Director for a Nonprofit Agency: A Step-by-Step Guide," *Popular Government* 65(4) (Summer 2000): 25.

4. If it chooses to do so, the board may solicit input from county social services employees, the county manager, or other knowledgeable persons.

5. In developing this profile, the board should focus on the anticipated needs of the department, not the strengths and weaknesses of the current or former social services director. "If a board focuses too much on correcting . . . [the] weaknesses [of the current or former social services director], it risks overcompensating for attributes that might not be most critical to the demands of the [director's] job. Listing the issues facing the agency helps the board shift its focus from the past to the future." Jenne and Henderson, "Hiring a Director for a Nonprofit Agency: A Step-by-Step Guide," 26–27.

6. The length of time involved in appointing a new director depends on many different factors. It might be as little as a few weeks if the board decides to promote an assistant social services director who has been groomed to succeed a retiring social services director, or as long as a year or more if the board decides to conduct an extensive search, if there is a shortage of suitable candidates, or if there are other complicating factors.

7. State rules require that the board's procedures for recruiting and selecting a new county social services director be validly related to the duties and responsibilities of the director's position and applied consistently to all applicants. 25 N.C. Admin. Code 01I .1905(a).

8. *See* 25 N.C. Admin. Code 01I .2002(e) and (g). An acting or interim social services director has the same powers and duties as a permanent social services director. *See In re* Brunswick County, 81 N.C. App. 391, 344 S.E.2d 584 (1986).

9. An emergency appointment may be made when an emergency situation exists requiring the services of an employee before it is possible to identify a qualified applicant through the regular selection process. When it is determined that an emergency appointment is necessary, all other requirements for appointments are waived.

10. 25 N.C. Admin. Code 01I .1902.

11. *Id.*

12. If applications are screened by the board or a subcommittee of the board during an official meeting of the board or subcommittee, the screening should be done in a closed session pursuant to G.S. 143-318.11(a)(6).

13. If a social services director does not meet these requirements, he or she must have a bachelor's degree in social work and three years of supervisory experience in the delivery of client services, one of which must have been in social services; have graduated from a four-year college or university and have had at least three years of supervisory experience in the delivery of client services, two of which must have been in social services; or have an equivalent combination of training and experience.

14. N.C. Office of State Personnel website (www.osp.state.nc.us/CLASS_SPECS/ Spec_Folder_09000-09999/PDF_Files/09929.pdf).

15. If the board or a subcommittee of the board reviews applications, the review should be done in a closed session pursuant to G.S. 143-318.11(a)(6).

16. The state Open Meetings Law is discussed in Chapter 10 of this handbook.

17. The board's selection procedures and methods must be validly related to the duties and responsibilities of the position, and the same selection process must be used consistently with all applicants. 25 N.C. Admin. Code 01I .1905(a).

18. Federal and state employment discrimination laws that apply to local governments are discussed in detail in Chapters 1, 4, 5, 6, and 7 of Stephen Allred, *Employment Law: A Guide for North Carolina Public Employers* (Chapel Hill: Institute of Government, The University of North Carolina at Chapel Hill, 1999).

19. *See* G.S. 153A-98; Elkin Tribune v. Yadkin County, 331 N.C. 735, 417 S.E.2d 465 (1992).

20. 25 N.C. Admin. Code 01I .1905.

21. *Id.*

22. *See* G.S. 128-15 and G.S. 126-83; Davis v. Vance County Dep't of Soc. Servs., 91 N.C. App. 428, 372 S.E.2d 88 (1988); Wright v. Blue Ridge Mental Health Auth., 134 N.C. App. 668, 518 S.E.2d 772 (1999).

23. G.S. 143-318.11(a)(6).

24. G.S. 108A-9(1); G.S. 108A-12. The board of county commissioners, however, must approve the amount of the director's salary. G.S. 108A-13.

25. 25 N.C. Admin. Code 01I .2002(a).

26. G.S. 108A-13.

27. N.C. Office of State Personnel website (www.osp.state.nc.us/ExternalHome/ Group5/LocalGovmt/0607SalaryPlan/guidelines.pdf). In 2008 the annual salaries of county social services directors in North Carolina ranged from about $44,000 to $155,000. *County Salaries in North Carolina 2009* (Chapel Hill: School of Government, The University of North Carolina at Chapel Hill, 2009) (www.sog.unc.edu/pubs/ electronicversions/pdfs/cosal2009/health.pdf).

28. G.S. 108A-9(3).

29. Suggested procedures and guidelines for a board's evaluation of its chief executive officer are discussed in Margaret S. Carlson, "'How Are We Doing?' Evaluating the Performance of the Chief Administrator," *Popular Government* 59(3) (Winter 1994): 24–29, and Margaret S. Carlson, "Board-Manager Performance Evaluations: Questions and Answers," *Popular Government* 62(4): (Summer 1997) 50–55.

30. By promising confidentiality to others when collecting information for an evaluation, board members may place themselves in the awkward position of having information about the director's performance that they can't use or share with the director or can only share in such a general way that it's not helpful.

31. *See* G.S. 153A-98.

32. *See* G.S. 108A-12(a).

33. See G.S. 126-1.1 as amended by S.L. 2007-372, superseding the decision in *Early v. Durham County Department of Social Services*, 172 N.C. App. 344, 616 S.E.2d 553 (2005), and former G.S. 126-35(a). Unless otherwise noted, the discussion in this chapter regarding the board's dismissal of the county social services director applies only with respect to directors who have attained career status.

34. *See* G.S. 126-5(a)(2); G.S. 126-35; G.S. 126-34; and G.S. 126-34.1. *See also* 25 N.C. Admin. Code 01I .2301. Unacceptable personal conduct and unsatisfactory job performance are not mutually exclusive categories. Depending on the facts of the particular situation, a director's conduct or performance may constitute unacceptable personal conduct and unsatisfactory job performance. A disciplinary action is not invalid simply because the board mischaracterizes the director's conduct or performance as unacceptable personal conduct rather than unsatisfactory job performance or vice versa.

35. 25 N.C. Admin. Code 01I .2302(a). *See also* Walker v. Dep't of Human Res., 100 N.C. App. 498, 397 S.E.2d 350 (1990).

36. 25 N.C. Admin. Code 01I .2303(a).

37. 25 N.C. Admin. Code 01I .2304(b).

38. The board must dismiss a director for unacceptable personal conduct if the board determines that the director was determined qualified and selected on the basis of falsified work experience or educational qualifications and, in all other cases involving post-hiring discovery of false or misleading information, must give the director a written warning, suspend the director without pay, reduce the director's salary, or dismiss the director. 25 N.C. Admin. Code 01I .2309(d).

39. If the board determines that the director was selected on the basis of falsified information or credentials related to work experience, education, credentialing, or licensure

requirements, the board must dismiss the director rather than taking less severe disciplinary action. 25 N.C. Admin. Code 01I .2309(d).

40. The state Open Meetings Law and closed sessions are discussed in Chapter 10 of this handbook.

41. G.S. 143-318.11(a)(6).

42. Unacceptable personal conduct must be corrected immediately. If the warning does not state the time in which the director must correct his or her job performance, he or she must do so within sixty days. 25 N.C. Admin. Code 01I .2305(a)(4).

43. 25 N.C. Admin. Code 01I .2305. The director may appeal a written warning only if the county's personnel ordinance or grievance procedure allows employees to appeal disciplinary warnings as well as more severe disciplinary actions (e.g., suspension without pay, demotion, or dismissal).

44. 25 N.C. Admin. Code 01I .2306(a); 25 N.C. Admin. Code 01I .2307. The board may place the director on investigatory status (remove the director from work status with pay) when such action is necessary to investigate allegations of performance or conduct deficiencies that would constitute just cause for disciplinary action, to provide time within which to schedule and conduct a pre-disciplinary conference, or to avoid disruption of the workplace or to protect the safety of persons or property. 25 N.C. Admin. Code 01I .2309(c).

45. 25 N.C. Admin. Code 01I .2306(a); 25 N.C. Admin. Code 01I .2307. A disciplinary action generally becomes "inactive" and may not serve as the basis for further disciplinary action when the reasons for the disciplinary action have been resolved or corrected or when the director does not have another active disciplinary action within eighteen months following the action. 25 N.C. Admin. Code 01I .2309(b).

46. 25 N.C. Admin. Code 01I .2304.

47. 25 N.C. Admin. Code 01I .2302(c). A previous disciplinary action may not be used to support the dismissal of a social services director for unsatisfactory job performance if the board notes in the director's personnel file that the reason for the disciplinary action has been resolved or corrected or if eighteen months have passed since the action, additional disciplinary action has not been taken against the director during the past eighteen months, and the board did not, before the expiration of the eighteen-month period, extend the period and give the director written notice of the reasons for extending the period. 25 N.C. Admin. Code 01I .2309(b).

48. 25 N.C. Admin. Code 01I .2308(4)(a).

49. 25 N.C. Admin. Code 01I .2308(4)(d).

50. 25 N.C. Admin. Code 01I .2308(4)(a). The director must be given as much advance notice as is practical under the circumstances but never less than two hours before the pre-disciplinary conference. If the director is not at work, notice may be mailed via certified mail, return receipt requested, or by any other appropriate method ensuring documentation of delivery.

51. 25 N.C. Admin. Code 01I .2308(4)(e).

52. *Id.*

53. 25 N.C. Admin. Code 01I .2308(4)(d); 25 N.C. Admin. Code 01I .2308(4)(e). Security personnel may be present when, in the board's discretion, a need for security exists.

54. 25 N.C. Admin. Code 01I .2308(4)(f). The letter may not be sent before the beginning of the next business day following the conclusion of the pre-dismissal conference or after the end of the second business day following the completion of the pre-dismissal conference.

55. 25 N.C. Admin. Code 01I .2310(a). Disciplinary warnings may not be appealed unless allowed under the county's grievance policy for social services employees. 25 N.C. Admin. Code 01I .2309(e)(2). A director who is serving a probationary period following appointment does not have the right to file an appeal that claims that he or she was disciplined or dismissed without just cause. 25 N.C. Admin. Code 01I .2002(a)(3). A county social services director who is not a career employee may or may not have a right to appeal his or her dismissal pursuant to the county's personnel ordinance or policies.

56. 25 N.C. Admin. Code 01I .2010(a). A director who alleges discrimination in connection with disciplinary action may "bypass" the county grievance procedure and file an appeal with the North Carolina Office of Administrative Hearings within thirty days of receipt of notice of the suspension, demotion, or dismissal. 25 N.C. Admin. Code 01I .2010(b).

57. *See* G.S. 126-35(a); G.S. 150B-23.

58. *See* G.S. 150B-23(a). The board must send notice of the director's appeal to the county manager or the chair of the board of county commissioners by certified mail within fifteen days of the board's receipt of notice of the appeal. G.S. 126-37(c).

59. *See* G.S. 150B-32; G.S. 150B-33. Hearings are held in the county in which the director lives. *See* G.S. 150B-24.

60. *See* G.S. 150B-23(b). The county may intervene in the administrative proceeding within thirty days of the date it receives notice of the employee's appeal. *See* G.S. 126-37(c).

61. *See* G.S. 150B-25; G.S. 150B-27 (subpoenas); G.S. 150B-28 (discovery); G.S. 150B-29 (rules of evidence).

62. *See* G.S. 126-35(d); G.S. 150B-34(a).

63. The Administrative Law Judge's recommended decision must contain findings of fact that are based on the evidence presented at the hearing and conclusions of law that address the legal issues raised by the board and director. *See* G.S. 150B-34(a).

64. *See* G.S. 150B-36.

65. *See* G.S. 150B-36(b3). The commission generally is required to issue its decision within sixty days of the date it receives the record of the administrative hearing or within sixty days of the date of its last official meeting, whichever is longer. *See* G.S. 150B-44.

66. *See* G.S. 126-37. The commission's decisions in these cases are binding on the social services board and the county but, on petition by the board or county, are subject to judicial review under Article 4 of the Administrative Procedure Act.

67. *See* G.S. 126-37(b1).

68. *Id.*

69. *Id.* The board, however, is not required to make additional or alternate findings of fact or conclusions of law. *See* Cunningham v. Catawba County, 128 N.C. App. 70, 493 S.E.2d 82 (1997).

70. *See* G.S. 126-37(b2); G.S. 150B-43. The petition may be filed in Wake County or in the county in which the director resides. G.S. 150B-45.

71. *See* G.S. 150B-45. The county may intervene in the proceeding in superior court even if it failed to seek intervention in the administrative proceeding. *See* G.S. 126-37(c). The decision of the superior court, however, is binding on the county regardless of whether it intervenes.

72. *See* G.S. 150B-51(a).

73. *See* G.S. 150B-51(c).

74. *See* G.S. 150B-51(b)(5). *See also* Thompson v. Wake County Bd. of Educ., 292 N.C. 406, 233 S.E.2d 538 (1977); Lackey v. Dep't of Human Res., 306 N.C. 231, 293 S.E. 2d 171 (1982); General Motors v. Kinlaw, 78 N.C. App. 521, 338 S.E.2d 114 (1985); Leiphart v. N.C. Sch. of the Arts, 80 N.C. App. 339, 342 S.E.2d 914 (1986); ACT-UP Triangle v. Comm'n for Health Servs., 345 N.C. 699, 483 S.E.2d 388 (1997).

75. *See* G.S. 150B-51(b).

76. Conversely, the board or county may appeal a superior court judgment that reverses the board's decision.

77. *See* G.S. 126-34 and G.S. 126-34.1. The procedures for these grievances and appeals are similar, but not always identical, to the procedure for grievances and appeals involving disciplinary action. *See* G.S. 126-34; G.S. 126-34.1; G.S. 126-36; G.S. 126-36.2; 25 N.C. ADMIN. CODE 01I .2310(a); and 25 N.C. ADMIN. CODE 01I .2310(b). A person who has been denied employment with the county social services department in violation of the equal employment opportunity requirements of state law has the right to appeal the denial to the SPC. *See* G.S. 126-34.1(b); G.S. 126-36.1. County social services directors may have additional grievance rights under county personnel ordinances and policies.

78. This authority could be delegated by the board of county commissioners to the county social services board if the board of county commissioners chooses.

79. *See* G.S. 153A-82. Ninety-nine of North Carolina's one hundred counties have county managers.

80. G.S. 108A-14(a)(2); *In re* Brunswick County, 81 N.C. App. 391, 344 S.E.2d 584 (1986).

81. *Id.* If a county's personnel ordinance gives the social services board a role in reviewing the director's actions in a case that involves a grievance or appeal filed by a county social services employee, the board's decision is advisory only, and, subject to administrative or judicial review, the director retains final authority to promote, manage, discipline, or discharge all employees of the county social services department.

82. G.S. 126-5(a)(2)b. The State Personnel Act does not apply to a county's social services employees to the extent that the board of county commissioners has established and implemented a personnel system that the State Personnel Commission has determined is "substantially equivalent" to the state personnel requirements governing county social services employees. G.S. 126-11.

83. The applicability of the State Personnel Act to county social services employees is discussed in more detail in Chapter 8 of John L. Saxon, *Social Services in North Carolina* (Chapel Hill: School of Government, The University of North Carolina at Chapel Hill, 2008).

84. G.S. 126-9(a).

85. G.S. 153A-94. If the county fails to file its rules regarding vacation and sick leave with the State Personnel Director, the leave provisions adopted under the State Personnel Act, rather than the county's leave policies, will apply to county social services employees. State law also authorizes the board of county commissioners to determine whether health insurance, life insurance, retirement benefits, or other employee fringe benefits will be provided to county employees (including social services employees).

86. The appointment, retention, and hiring of attorneys to provide legal services to the county social services department is discussed in detail in Chapter 9 of Saxon, *Social Services in North Carolina*. Chapter 12 of this handbook discusses legal representation of social services board members who are sued in their individual or official capacities in connection with civil tort claims.

Chapter 9

The Board's Responsibilities Regarding Social Services Policy, Administration, and Funding

Until the 1960s county social services boards exercised a significant amount of authority and responsibility with respect to administering and establishing policies for public assistance and social services programs in North Carolina.

Since the 1960s, however, the number, scope, size, and complexity of public assistance and social services programs have grown dramatically; the size and professionalism of county social services staffs have increased; and the responsibility and authority of the federal and state governments regarding social services programs have grown relative to that of counties. As a result, responsibility and authority regarding many aspects of social services programs have shifted more or less steadily over time from the county board of social services to the county director of social services, to state social services agencies, and to the federal government.

Social services boards, however, retain some authority and responsibility regarding social services policy, funding, and administration. And in order to effectively discharge these responsibilities, social services board members need a working knowledge of how social services programs are administered and funded, the types of assistance and services these programs provide to county residents, and who is eligible for the assistance and services provided by the county social services department.[1]

Advising Local Public Officials

One of the most important, but frequently overlooked, responsibilities of the county social services board is to advise local public officials about social and economic problems in the community and to assist local officials in developing plans and policies to improve social and economic conditions in the county.[2]

To adequately discharge this responsibility, county social services board members first must educate themselves about all of the social and economic problems that affect their community, not just the problems that are the focus of public assistance and social services programs administered by the county social services department or problems that affect families and people with limited incomes and financial resources. Social services boards, therefore, should be concerned about

- unemployment, job training, and economic development;
- crime, juvenile delinquency, and gang activity;
- homelessness;
- domestic violence;
- lack of available or affordable housing, transportation, health care, or recreation;
- adolescent pregnancy;
- out-of-wedlock births;
- school dropout rates;
- child abuse and neglect;
- abuse, neglect, and exploitation of elderly or disabled adults;
- hunger; and
- poverty.

Some of the ways that county social services boards and board members can educate themselves about social and economic problems in their communities include

- seeking information, data, statistics, and reports from the county social services director, other public agencies or officials (including law enforcement agencies, public schools, and health departments), community organizations, community leaders, local experts, and informed citizens;

- holding roundtable discussions with public officials and agencies and community organizations;
- holding public hearings to solicit public comment and input about particular issues or problems;
- establishing board subcommittees or advisory committees or task forces to investigate particular issues or problems;
- cooperating in the establishment of interagency or community task forces to investigate particular issues or problems;
- requesting public or private agencies to conduct community studies and public surveys;
- visiting community organizations, jails, job-training centers, schools, senior centers, Smart Start and Head Start programs, community action agencies, recreation centers, churches, civic organizations, public housing projects, and public and private human services agencies;
- talking with and listening to county residents one-on-one; and
- staying informed about events in the county and staying in touch with a broad cross-section of the community.

In addition to educating themselves about the social and economic problems in their communities, social services boards and board members need to

- learn about the causes of the problems;
- identify the ways in which the problems have been successfully or unsuccessfully addressed by public and private agencies and organizations around the nation;
- identify the resources that are available and would be needed to address the problems locally;
- identify the officials, agencies, and organizations that are responsible for addressing those problems or have the authority, power, and resources to do so;
- assist local public officials, agencies, and others in developing plans and policies to address those problems; and
- advocate for the adoption, implementation, and funding of plans and policies to address the problems.

Establishing Local Social Services Policies

State law authorizes the county social services board to adopt policies regarding county-funded programs for the care of indigent persons.[3] As a practical matter, though, the board's authority to adopt policies for county-funded social services programs is subject to that of the board of county commissioners, which can determine local social services policies through its decision to fund or not fund county social services programs and attach conditions to the use of county funding for those programs.

State law also authorizes the county social services board to establish local policies for the Work First program, the State-County Special Assistance program, the Food and Nutrition Services program, the Foster Care and Adoption Assistance programs, the Medicaid program, and other public assistance or social services programs established by Chapter 108A of the North Carolina General Statutes[4] (hereinafter G.S.). If the board does so, however, its policies must be consistent with applicable federal and state laws and regulations regarding the administration of those public assistance and social services programs, eligibility for assistance and services under those programs, and the nature, amount, scope, and duration of assistance and services provided under the programs.[5] And because federal and state rules that govern state and federal–state social services programs are so detailed and comprehensive, the board's authority to adopt local policies regarding state and federal–state social services programs is actually quite limited.

In addition, state law and rules authorize the county social services board to

- approve (along with the board of county commissioners) the social services director's plan for charging fees for services provided voluntarily by the county social services department to public or private agencies or individuals;[6]
- adopt rules regarding the conveyance of surplus government-owned automobiles to persons who receive assistance under the Work First program;[7]
- determine the types of transportation that will be provided to persons who receive transportation services, community living services, adult day care services, employment and training support services, and health support services from the county social services department under the Social Services Block Grant (SBBG);[8]
- adopt a waiting list policy for services provided under the SSBG;[9]

- determine whether the county social services department will use the declaration or verification method of establishing financial eligibility for services provided under the SSBG;[10] and
- assist in the development of the county's Work First plan.[11]

Monitoring and Evaluating Social Services Programs

Under state law the county social services board is responsible for consulting with the social services director regarding issues that affect the county social services department and assisting the director in planning the department's budget.[12] In order to discharge these responsibilities, the board must exercise at least some responsibility for the general direction, oversight, and evaluation of the social services department and the public assistance and social services programs it administers. One way social services boards do this is to work with the county social services director, state social services employees, and others to

- establish a clear vision to guide the work of the county social services board, director, and department;
- adopt a statement that articulates the department's mission;
- establish desired outcomes or results that the department will seek to achieve; and
- periodically measure and evaluate the department's success in achieving those outcomes or results.[13]

Social services boards also are involved in the monitoring and evaluation of child protective services through the social services board chair's appointment of one social services board member to serve as a member of the county's community child protection team. The team is responsible for reviewing selected cases involving children who are receiving child protective services from the county social services department, reviewing all cases in which a child has died as a result of suspected abuse and neglect within twelve months after the child or the child's family received child protective services or within twelve months after a report was made to the social services department regarding the abuse or neglect of the child or another child in the family, and submitting an annual report and recommendations to the board of county commissioners that identify gaps and deficiencies in the provision of child protective services, the resources needed to protect children from abuse and neglect, and suggested improvements to the child protective services system.[14]

Administering Social Services Programs

State law requires every county social services board to appoint a county social services director who is responsible for[15]

- administering the state and federal–state social services programs established by G.S. Chapter 108A in accordance with applicable federal and state rules;[16]
- assessing reports of child abuse and neglect and taking appropriate action to protect abused, neglected, or dependent children pursuant to North Carolina's Juvenile Code;[17]
- accepting children for placement in foster homes and supervising foster care placements;[18]
- investigating proposed adoptive placements and supervising adoptive placements;[19]
- filing legal proceedings seeking termination of parental rights with respect to certain juveniles placed in the custody of the department of social services;[20]
- receiving and evaluating reports of abuse, neglect, or exploitation of disabled adults and taking appropriate action to protect disabled adults from abuse, neglect, or exploitation;[21]
- supervising the operation of adult care homes;[22]
- conducting and making decisions in local hearings in appeals by persons who have applied for or are receiving public assistance or social services;[23]
- reviewing requests for expunction from the list of persons who have been determined to be responsible for the abuse or serious neglect of a juvenile;[24]
- serving as the guardian for incapacitated adults when required to do so by the clerk of superior court;[25]
- serving on the local community child protection or child fatality prevention team;[26]
- serving on the county's juvenile crime prevention council;[27]
- arranging for the burial or cremation of unclaimed bodies of deceased persons;[28]

- issuing certificates that authorize the employment of youth between the ages of twelve and eighteen in accordance with applicable federal and state child labor laws;[29]
- performing emergency management functions specified under local emergency management plans;[30]
- acting as the agent of the state Social Services Commission and the state Department of Health and Human Services (DHHS) with respect to their work in the county;[31] and
- performing other powers and duties specified by state law.[32]

Under state law, the county social services director and his or her staff, not the county social services board, are primarily responsible for administering county, state, and federal–state public assistance and social services programs for county residents.

State laws and policies, however, authorize the county social services board to determine whether

- an individual meets the eligibility requirements for State-County Special Assistance (or delegate that responsibility to the social services director);[33]
- an individual meets the eligibility requirements for the state's Medicaid program (or delegate that responsibility to the social services director);[34]
- a family that is subject to the Work First time limit will be granted an extension due to hardship;
- a person who has applied for or received State-County Special Assistance has committed fraud and, if so, what action should be taken by the county social services department;[35]
- a person who has applied for or received assistance under the Low-Income Energy Assistance program or the Crisis Intervention program has committed fraud, and, if so, what action should be taken by the county social services department.[36]

State law also requires county social services boards to provide investigative assistance to district attorneys regarding reports about the abandonment or failure to support certain dependent children or the misuse of Work First Family Assistance.[37]

Social services board members should remember that the social services director and staff, not the board, are responsible for administering the public assistance and social services programs offered through the county social services department. The board's focus, therefore, should be on the impact social services programs have on county residents and community well-being, not the day-to-day administrative procedures or detailed month-to-month statistics regarding the administration of those programs.

Examining Social Services Records

State law authorizes the county social services board and social services board members to examine the social services department's records regarding individuals and families who have applied for or are receiving public assistance or social services as well as any other information held by the department regarding the provision of public assistance or social services to county residents.[38] The board and board members, however, should do so only when they need access to agency records or information in order to discharge their official responsibilities, and they may not use or publicly disclose confidential information contained in social services records except as specifically authorized by law.[39]

Approving Social Services Contracts

G.S. 108A-10 authorizes the county social services board to enter into contracts with any public or private agency or individual under which the county social services department will voluntarily render social services to or for the agency or person in exchange for a fee to cover the cost of the services.[40] Contracts under G.S. 108A-10, however, are relatively rare and do not include contracts under which the county social services department purchases or leases real property, office space, automobiles, computers, office supplies, or the like; purchases professional or business services for the department; or contracts with public or private entities to provide child care, child support, transportation, medical care, housing, job training, or other social services on behalf of the department to individuals who have applied and are eligible for public assistance or social services programs offered through the county social services department.

State law also authorizes social services boards to enter into agreements with counties or municipalities to undertake or carry out specified community development activities on behalf of the county or city.[41]

Apart from its authority under those laws, however, the county social services board generally has no legal authority to enter into any type of legal contract on behalf of the board or the county social services department. Instead, state law provides that the residents of each county are a "body politic and corporate," that, as a corporate entity, each county has the authority to "contract and be contracted with," and that, except as otherwise provided by law, the county's corporate authority, including the authority to enter into contract, must be exercised by or through the county's elected board of commissioners.[42] Thus, as a general rule, all contracts that involve the county and county agencies and boards, including the county social services department and board, must be approved by the board of county commissioners or a public official (usually the county manager, the county purchasing officer, or county department heads) designated by the board.[43]

Developing, Approving, and Administering the Social Services Budget

Because the county social services department is an agency of the county government and is not an independent unit of local government or public authority, state law requires that the county's social services budget be included in the county budget ordinance that is adopted by the board of county commissioners pursuant to the requirements of the Local Government Budget and Fiscal Control Act (LGBFCA).[44] The board of county commissioners, therefore, has the ultimate authority and responsibility, within the parameters set by state law, to determine the size of the county's budget for social services, to levy the local taxes that will be used with federal and state funding to provide public assistance and social services to county residents, and to specify the purposes for which the county social services department may use budgeted public funds.[45]

This does not mean, though, that the county social services board has no role or responsibility with respect to the county's social services budget. State law expressly requires the county social services board to "assist [the county social services director] in planning budgets for the county department of social services" and to "transmit or present" the department's budget to the board of county commissioners.[46]

To assist counties in planning their social services budgets, G.S. 108A-88 requires the state DHHS, by February 15 of each year, to notify each county social services director, county manager, and board of county commissioners of

- the amount of state and federal funds estimated to be available to the counties for public assistance and social services programs and related administrative costs for the next fiscal year and
- the percentage of county financial participation expected to be required for each program.[47]

Every county's proposed social services budget, however, contains more than the amounts indicated in the state DHHS estimates for mandated programs. In the areas of child welfare and child protective services, for example, federal and state funds available to the county, along with any county match required to receive those funds, generally are insufficient to carry out the county's legal responsibilities with respect to abused, neglected, and dependent juveniles and therefore must be supplemented with additional county funding. Similarly, some state mandates, such as the requirement that a county social services director serve as guardian for incompetent adults when appointed by the court to do so, do not include designated sources of state funding and must be paid from county funds if other federal or state funding is not available. In addition, county social services departments sometimes provide nonmandated assistance and services to meet local needs and these optional services must be supported by county funding to the extent that other federal or state funding is unavailable.

Under the LGBFCA, the county social services director must submit to the county manager,[48] by April 30 or such earlier date as determined by the county manager,[49] a proposed budget that includes

- the department's request for county appropriations for the coming fiscal year;
- an estimate of departmental revenues for the coming year (including federal, state, and nonpublic funding);
- actual and estimated expenditures for each category of expenditure included in the county budget ordinance for the current and immediately preceding fiscal years;[50]
- actual and estimated amounts realized for each source of revenue for the current and immediately preceding fiscal years;[51] and
- any additional information requested by the manager.

The LGBFCA requires the county budget officer to prepare a proposed budget for the county (including the county department of social services) and submit it to the board of county commissioners by June 1. The manager's proposed budget may increase, decrease, or revise the proposed budget submitted by the county social services director without the approval or consent of the social services director or board.

After the proposed county budget is submitted to the board of county commissioners, the board must hold a public hearing on the proposed budget and adopt, no later than July 1, a budget ordinance that

- accepts or modifies the manager's proposed budget;
- makes appropriations of county revenues for specified purposes, functions, activities, or objectives;[52]
- appropriates sufficient funds to pay the county's share of mandated public assistance and social services programs;[53]
- levies the county property tax for the coming fiscal year;[54]
- includes a statement of the county's estimated revenues for the coming fiscal year;[55] and
- is balanced.[56]

Under state law, the county social services director is responsible for administering "funds provided by the board of [county] commissioners for the care of indigent persons in the county . . . ."[57] State law, however, also requires that the expenditures by the county social services department be made in accordance with the LGBFCA, prohibits the expenditure of funds by county agencies unless the expenditure has been authorized under the county budget ordinance, requires that all county revenues and expenditures be accounted for through the establishment of an accounting system that uses generally accepted accounting principles, requires the pre-auditing of all financial obligations, requires the review and approval of all disbursements by county agencies, and establishes requirements regarding financial reporting and audits.[58]

The county social services board, therefore, does not have the legal authority to approve or disapprove the county's social services budget, to determine the size of the budget, to levy the local taxes or provide the funding that will be used to provide public assistance and social services to county residents, to determine the purposes for which the county social services department may use budgeted public funds, to administer the county's social services budget, or to expend public funding for social services.

The social services board, however, can and should help shape the county's social services budget by working with the social services director, the county manager, the county commissioners, other state and local government officials, and the community to ensure that adequate public funding is available for the public assistance and social services programs that county residents need and that public funding for social services is used efficiently and effectively to improve the lives of county residents, improve the community's well-being, and achieve the mission and goals of the county social services department.

Notes

1. Public assistance and social services programs are discussed in detail in Chapter 11 of John L. Saxon, *Social Services in North Carolina* (Chapel Hill: School of Government, The University of North Carolina at Chapel Hill, 2008). The funding of public assistance and social services programs is discussed in detail in Chapter 12 of Saxon, *Social Services in North Carolina*.

2. *See* N.C. GEN. STAT. § 108A-9(2) (hereinafter G.S.).

3. G.S. 108A-14(a)(4). These programs do not include state or federal–state social services programs that are funded in part by county tax revenues.

4. G.S. 108A-1. In counties designated by the General Assembly as "electing" counties under G.S. 108A-27.3, the board of county commissioners, rather than the county social services board, is authorized to adopt local policies for the county's Work First program.

5. G.S. 108A-1.

6. G.S. 108A-10.

7. G.S. 160A-279(a).

8. 10A N.C. ADMIN. CODE 71I.0101.

9. 10A N.C. ADMIN. CODE 71R.0803(b)(1).

10. 10A N.C. ADMIN. CODE 71R.0701.

11. *See* G.S. 108A-27.3(c) and G.S. 108A-27.6(c) (requiring the board of county commissioners to appoint at least one member of the county social services board to a committee to develop the county's Work First plan).

12. G.S. 108A-9(3).

13. A number of county social services boards participate in the "Leading by Results" program developed by the North Carolina Association of County Directors of Social Services. The UNC School of Government also offers a number of resources regarding program evaluation, performance management, and benchmarking.

14. G.S. 7B-1407(b)(6); G.S. 7B-1406(a).

15. G.S. 108A-12; G.S. 108A-14. Although state law allows two or more county social services boards to appoint by joint action one person to serve as the social services director for all of those counties, no social services boards currently do so. *See* G.S. 108A-12(b).

16. G.S. 108A-14(a)(3). These programs include, but are not limited to, Work First, Medicaid, Food and Nutrition Services (Food Stamps), State-County Special Assistance, Low-Income Energy Assistance, and Foster Care and Adoption Assistance. In "electing" counties, the board of county commissioners may direct that the Work First program be administered by a public official or public or private entity other than the county social services director and department. G.S. 108A-27(f); G.S. 108A-27.3(b).

17. G.S. 108A-14(a)(11). *See also* G.S. 7B-300; G.S. 7B-302; G.S. 7B-307; G.S. 7B-320; G.S. 7B-500.

18. G.S. 108A-14(a)(12). *See also* G.S. 7B-505; G.S. 7B-903; G.S. 7B-904; G.S. 7B-905; G.S. 7B-910; G.S. 7B-1905; G.S. 7B-2503; G.S. 7B-2506.

19. G.S. 108A-14(a)(6); G.S. 108A-14(a)(13). *See also* G.S. 48-1-109; G.S. 48-2-501; G.S. 48-3-201; G.S. 48-3-203; G.S. 48-3-204; G.S. 48-3-303; G.S. 48-3-309; G.S. 48-3-601.

20. G.S. 7B-1103.

21. G.S. 108A-14(a)(14). *See also* G.S. 108A-103 through 108A-106; G.S. 108A-108; G.S. 108A-109.

22. G.S. 108A-14(a)(8). *See also* G.S. 131D-2(b); G.S. 131D-26.

23. G.S. 108A-79(f).

24. G.S. 7B-321.

25. G.S. 108A-15; G.S. 35A-1201(4); G.S. 35A-1213(d).

26. G.S. 7B-1407(b)(1); G.S. 7B-1409.

27. G.S. 143B-544(a)(7).

28. G.S. 130A-415.

29. G.S. 95-25.5; G.S. 108A-14(a)(7).

30. *See* G.S. 166A-7.

31. G.S. 108A-14(a)(5).

32. In exercising these powers and duties, the director may delegate to one or more staff of the county social services department the authority to act as the director's representative and may limit the delegated authority of his or her representative to specific tasks or areas of expertise. G.S. 108A-14(b). Ultimately, however, the county social services director remains responsible and accountable for the administration of the department and the actions of the department's staff.

33. G.S. 108A-43(a).

34. 10A N.C. Admin. Code 21B .0205(b).

35. 10A N.C. Admin. Code 71P .0508(e). Fraud is defined as the willful and knowing provision of incorrect or misleading information in connection with an individual's application for assistance, the willful and knowing failure to report changes that affect the amount of assistance payable to an individual, or the willful and knowing failure to report the receipt of assistance to which an individual is not entitled. If the board determines that a person has committed fraud, it may direct the county social services director to take no action (in unusual cases or cases involving hardship), take administrative action to recover an overpayment of assistance, file a civil lawsuit to attempt to recover the overpayment, or ask the district attorney to initiate a criminal prosecution.

36. 10A N.C. Admin. Code 71V .0107 and 10A N.C. Admin. Code 71V .0204.

37. *See* G.S. 15-155.2(a)(1).

38. G.S. 108A-11.

39. G.S. 108A-11; G.S. 108A-80. Rules regarding the confidentiality of information contained in county social services records is discussed in detail in Chapter 13 of Saxon, *Social Services in North Carolina*.

40. The board may, if it chooses, delegate this authority to the county social services director.

41. *See* G.S. 153A-376(b) and G.S. 160A-456(b).

42. *See* G.S. 153A-11 and G.S. 153A-12.

43. The board of county commissioners could, of course, authorize the social services board to approve contracts that involve the county social services department. But if this is not the case, the social services board has no role or responsibility with respect to the approval of contracts other than those made pursuant to G.S. 108A-10.

44. The Local Government Budget and Fiscal Control Act (LGBFCA) and social services budgets and funding are discussed in Chapter 12 of Saxon, *Social Services in North Carolina*.

45. *See* G.S. 159-8(a); G.S. 108A-90; G.S. 153A-149(b)(8); G.S. 153A-149(c)(30); G.S. 153A-255.

46. G.S. 108A-9(3); G.S. 108A-9(4). State law, however, does not require the board to approve the proposed budget for the county social services department, does not give the board the authority to disapprove the director's proposed budget, and does not give the board any express authority with respect to administering the department's budget or funds.

47. In providing estimates to the counties in odd-numbered years, the state Department of Health and Human Services (DHHS) must include notification of any changes in public assistance funding levels, formulas, or programs that the governor has proposed to the General Assembly under the Executive Budget Act. Counties also must be notified of changes in the proposed budget of the governor and the Advisory Budget Commission that result from action by the General Assembly or Congress subsequent to the February 15 estimates. The initial estimates that counties receive usually are revised several times. DHHS budget estimates are posted on the Division of Social Services' website (www.dhhs. state.nc.us/dss/budget/estimates.htm).

48. In ninety-nine of North Carolina's one hundred counties, the county manager is the county budget officer. *See* G.S. 159-9. References in this section to the county manager refer to the county manager or other county official who is the county budget officer.

49. All North Carolina counties currently require that proposed departmental budgets be submitted to the budget officer before April 30.

50. This information may be submitted by the county finance office rather than the county social services director. *See* G.S. 159-10.

51. This information may be submitted by the county finance office rather than the county social services director. *See* G.S. 159-10

52. G.S. 159-7(b)(2). Appropriations may be made for specified object classes within each county department or agency, as a lump sum for each department or agency, or for broad programs that include two or more departments or agencies. Most county budget ordinances make appropriations on a departmental basis. A county budget ordinance, however, may require a county department to spend its appropriation for the purposes specified in the more detailed budget upon which the budget ordinance was based.

53. G.S. 108A-90.

54. G.S. 159-7(b)(2) and G.S. 159-13(c).

55. All expenditures from revenues received by the county or county departments, other than those for capital or grant projects and those accounted for in internal service or trust or agency funds, must be authorized by the county budget ordinance. County budget ordinances, therefore, include appropriations from federal and state funds received by the county for public assistance and social services programs as well as appropriations for these programs from county tax revenues. They do not include public assistance payments made by the state directly to or on behalf of county residents. In fact about half of the total amount budgeted for social services by all North Carolina counties is paid from federal and state funding, and only half of it is funded by county tax revenues.

56. G.S. 159-8(a). "A budget ordinance is balanced when the sum of estimated net revenues and appropriated fund balances is equal to appropriations." G.S. 159-8(a).

57. G.S. 108A-14(a)(4).

58. These and other provisions of the LGBFCA are discussed in more detail in David M. Lawrence, *Local Government Finance in North Carolina* (Chapel Hill: Institute of Government, The University of North Carolina at Chapel Hill, 1990). Under the LGB-FCA, the county finance officer is legally responsible for establishing and maintaining the county's accounting system, for pre-auditing obligations, reviewing and approving disbursements, managing cash and other assets, and preparing financial reports. The finance officer's responsibilities with respect to the county social services budget, however, may be delegated to and exercised by the county social services director or a special deputy county finance officer employed by the county social services department.

Chapter 10

Social Services Board Meetings and Procedures

Although county social services board members perform some of their responsibilities as individuals, the authority, powers, duties, and responsibilities of the county social services board are vested in the entire board—not individual social services board members—and may be exercised by the board only when its members act together as a public body. Official meetings of the board, therefore, are the means by which board members act together as a public body to exercise the board's authority, powers, duties, and responsibilities.

Legal Requirements

State law requires the county social services board to meet at least once each month and more often if additional meetings are called by the board chair.[1]

In addition all official meetings of the board and board committees must be held in accordance with the requirements of the state's Open Meetings Law, which are discussed in the following sections of this chapter.[2]

Frequency, Date, Time, and Location of Board Meetings

As noted above, state law requires the county social services board to meet at least once during each calendar month of the year.[3] The board, however, should meet as often as is necessary to perform its work. And if the board cannot accomplish all of its work during its monthly meetings, it should hold additional, special meetings as needed.[4]

Social services boards may, by majority vote, determine the dates and times of their monthly board meetings.[5] Although they are not required to do so, most social services boards establish a regular date and time for monthly board meetings (for example, the first Wednesday of each month at 7:00 PM). But regardless of whether or not the board establishes a regular meeting date and time, the board should consider the schedules and availability of board members and the county social services director and staff along with the interests of the public and persons who may be interested in attending board meetings when it determines its meeting schedule.

Social services boards also have the authority to determine the location at which they will meet. Although social services board meetings often are held at the county social services department, the board may meet at other locations in or beyond the county if it chooses to do so. All board meetings, however, should be held at a place that is conveniently located for those who will be attending, has adequate parking and is accessible via public transportation, is accessible to persons with disabilities, is safe, is large enough, provides sufficient seating and can be arranged to comfortably and appropriately accommodate all the people who will attend board meetings, has access to any audio-visual equipment that may be required, has good lighting, acoustics, heating, cooling, and ventilation, and has access to adequate public restrooms, water fountains, and other necessary facilities.

Public Notice of Official Meetings

North Carolina's Open Meetings Law requires the county social services board to give public notice of all of its official meetings (including those at which all of the board's business will be conducted in closed session) as well as the official meetings of committees or subcommittees of the board.[6]

An official board meeting is the "meeting, assembly, or gathering together at any time or place or the simultaneous communication by conference telephone or other electronic means of a majority of the members of" the board for the purpose of conducting a hearing, participating in deliberations, voting or taking official action, or otherwise transacting public business.[7]

The type of public notice that must be given for social services board meetings depends on whether the meeting is a regular board meeting, a special board meeting, an emergency meeting, or a recessed meeting.[8]

A regular social services board meeting is a meeting held on the regular date and at the regular time and place (for example, the second Tuesday of every month at 4:00 PM at the county social services director's office) specified in a notice filed with the clerk of the board of county commissioners.

If a social services board establishes a regular date, time, and place for its meetings, and the social services director, acting as the board's secretary, files the board's regular meeting schedule with the clerk of the county's board of commissioners, the board does not have to give any further public notice of any board meeting held at the regular date, time, and location.[9] Once filed, the regular meeting schedule adopted by the board remains in effect until it is changed by the board. If, however, the board makes any change with respect to its regular meeting date, time, or location, the social services director, acting as the board's secretary, must file notice of the board's amended regular meeting schedule with the clerk of the county's board of commissioners at least seven calendar days before the next regular board meeting that will be held under the amended meeting schedule.[10]

A "special" board meeting is any board meeting (other than an emergency or recessed meeting) that is held at a date, time, or place other than the regular date, time, or place for board meetings specified in the notice of regular board meetings on file with the clerk of the board of county commissioners. If, for example, the board regularly meets on the first Monday of the month but decides to meet on the second Monday in September (because of the Labor Day holiday) and then resume its regular schedule in October, the September board meeting is a special meeting. Or if the board chair calls an additional board meeting in May or the board decides to hold its regular meeting in June at a different location, those board meetings are special meetings.

Whenever a social services board holds a special meeting, the social services director, acting as the board's secretary, must post notice of the date, time, place, and purpose of the meeting on the principal bulletin board of the county department of social services or at the door of the board's usual meeting place at least forty-eight hours before the meeting and mail, fax, or deliver a copy of the notice to anyone who has requested, in writing, that he or she be provided with notice of special board meetings.[11]

If a social services board must hold a meeting in response to unexpected circumstances that require the board's immediate consideration, it may do so as soon as possible after providing notice, either in person or by phone, of the emergency meeting to any newspaper or radio or television station that has asked to receive notice of emergency board meetings.[12]

Election and Role of the Board Chair

State law requires each social services board to elect one of its members as the board chair and to do so annually during an open session of the board's July meeting.[13]

A social services board member who is elected as the board's chair serves as the chair for a term of one year, may be reelected for additional, consecutive one-year terms, and continues to serve as chair until his or her successor is elected.[14]

Although state law does not expressly authorize a social services board to designate one of its members as the board's vice-chair, a social services board may do so and may authorize its vice-chair to exercise the chair's powers and duties in the event of the chair's absence, disability, death, resignation, or removal from office.[15]

As noted above, state law expressly authorizes the board chair to call additional meetings of the board.[16] In addition the board's chair has the implied power and duty to preside at board meetings; to ensure that board meetings are conducted fairly, efficiently, and in accordance with the board's rules of procedure; to recognize members who wish to speak at board meetings; and to rule on motions and questions of procedure at board meetings.[17]

State law also gives the board chair (rather than the board as a whole) the legal authority to appoint a board member to the local community child protection team.[18]

A social services board chair also may function as the board's primary spokesperson, the primary link between the board and the social services director and between the board and other bodies, or the mediator of disputes among board members. To some extent, though, the role and responsibilities of the social services board chair vary from county to county, person to person, and time to time based on the traditions of each board and the personality and approach of each board chair. And for this reason, social services board members should discuss, on a regular basis, their understanding and expectations with respect to the chair's role and responsibilities.[19]

Agenda and Order of Business

Preparing, adopting, and following agendas for social services board meetings are the means by which a social services board can exercise self-discipline with respect to the matters it will consider, how it will consider those matters, and when and for how long it will consider those matters. As John Carver notes:

> Governing boards have precious little time in which to do their jobs. . . . There is little room for inappropriate or wasteful activity. . . . It is not acceptable to talk about any issue that might come up. It is not acceptable to talk about an issue in whatever way is desired. It is not acceptable to talk about an issue at an inappropriate time. . . . Boards cannot simply address any topics in any way they wish at the moment and hope to excel.[20]

Agendas for social services board meetings should focus on the board's work, and every item on the board's agenda should relate in some way to the board's role and responsibilities.[21] Carver, therefore, suggests that governing boards establish explicit policies governing the development and adoption of meeting agendas, that these policies include clear criteria for deciding what types of issues the board should consider, and that proposed agenda items that do not meet these criteria not be placed on the board's agenda.

Historically some county social services boards have allowed the county social services director to prepare the proposed agenda for social services board meetings. The dangers in this practice, however, are that, by relying too heavily on the social services director or staff, the agenda for social services board meetings will become the director's or staff's agenda rather than the board's agenda, that board meetings will focus on the director's or staff's work rather than the board's work, and that the board will become either too passive and dependent or inappropriately involved in micromanaging the work of the director and staff.[22] Therefore, unless otherwise provided by the board,

- the board chair should prepare a proposed agenda for each board meeting with input from the social services director and other board members and in accordance with the board's policies regarding meeting agendas and order of business;
- the director, acting as the board's secretary, should send a copy of the agenda and any additional information related to agenda items to social services board members at least two to five days before the meeting; and
- the board, as its first order of business at the meeting, should decide whether items should be added to or removed from the proposed agenda, make any additional changes to the proposed agenda, and adopt the agenda for the meeting.[23]

Agendas for county social services board meetings generally should follow a standard order of business that gives priority to items that require immediate consideration or action, allows routine or noncontroversial items to be handled expeditiously, and ensures that matters are not allowed to slip through the cracks or be placed on a back burner indefinitely.

Social services boards also should ensure that adequate time is allotted for every item on their agenda and that the time they spend on one or two agenda items does not displace other items that require the board's attention. The agendas adopted by some boards, for example, specify the amount of time for each agenda item. Board policies also should address the length of board meetings and what the board will do if there is insufficient time to consider all the items on its agenda.

The social service board should provide a copy of the board's agenda to persons attending board meetings. A board must provide a copy of the board's agenda to attendees if the board discusses or acts on matters by reference to a number, letter, or other designation of the matter on the board's agenda and attendees need a copy of the agenda to understand what is being deliberated, voted, or acted upon.[24]

More generally, though, the agendas of social services board meetings and all documents or records submitted to the board in connection with social services board meetings are public records and must be made available to any person, upon request, for inspection or copying except to the extent that they contain privileged or confidential information that may not be publicly disclosed under applicable state or federal laws.[25]

Rules of Procedure

County social services boards have the authority to establish local rules that govern the procedures they will follow in scheduling board meetings, determining the agendas for board meetings, conducting business at board meetings, appointing the third member of the social services board, electing the board chair, evaluating the board's work, and working together as board members.

By adopting written rules of procedure and following those rules, a social services board ensures a level playing field on which all of its members have an equal and fair opportunity to participate in the board's business. And when conflicts or crises arise, they should be resolved by reference to the board's rules rather than being decided on an ad hoc, arbitrary, or personal basis.

Apart from the state's Open Meetings Law, state law provides little guidance as to the procedures that social services boards must follow in connection with board meetings. Social services boards, therefore, have a fair amount of discretion to develop their own rules of procedure as long as those rules are not inconsistent with the requirements of the Open Meetings Law or other applicable statutes.

A board's rules of procedure, however, should be based upon and be consistent with the following principles of board governance:

- the board must act as a body;
- the board should proceed in the most efficient manner possible;
- the board must act by at least a majority vote;
- every board member must have an equal opportunity to participate in decision-making;
- the board's rules of procedure must be applied fairly and followed consistently;
- the board's actions should be the result of a decision on the merits and not a manipulation of procedural rules.[26]

The UNC School of Government has developed suggested rules of procedure for small local government boards that county social services boards can use as a resource to adopt their own rules of procedure.[27] These suggested rules incorporate the requirements of the state's Open Meetings Law, are consistent with the principles of board governance noted above, and include rules regarding board meetings, adoption of meeting agendas, the order of business for board meetings, the duties of the board chair, quorum, minutes, public hearings, appointments, committees, motions, debate, and voting.

Quorum and Voting

A county social services board may not take any official action or transact public business at a board meeting unless a quorum of the board's membership is present.[28] State law, however, does not specify the number of social services board members required to constitute a quorum of the board.

County social services boards, therefore, should adopt local rules of procedure and practice that specify the number of board members that will constitute a quorum, and, in the absence of local rules or practices, should consider a quorum to be a majority of the board's membership (at least two members of a three-member board or at least three members of a five-member board).[29]

Except as otherwise provided by state law or by a board's rules of procedure, all decisions by the county social services board should be made by majority vote of the members who are present and constitute a quorum at an official board meeting.[30] A board member who presides at a social services board meeting as the board's chair or vice-chair retains his or her right to vote with respect to all issues coming before the board but cannot cast a second vote to break a tie vote among the other board members.

North Carolina's Open Meetings Law prohibits county social services boards from taking some actions, including the appointment of the third social services board member and the appointment or dismissal of the county social services director during a closed session of an official board meeting.

In addition, the state Open Meetings Law prohibits social services board members from voting by secret ballot. The law, however, allows board members to vote by written ballot if the ballots are signed, the minutes of the board meeting show how each member voted, and the ballots are available for public inspection after the meeting.[31]

Recording and Public Comment

North Carolina's Open Meetings Law allows any person to photograph, film, tape-record, or otherwise reproduce any part of an open meeting of the county social services board and allows any radio or television station to broadcast all or any part of an open board meeting.[32] The board, however, may regulate the placement and use of recording or broadcasting equipment to the extent necessary to prevent undue interference with its meetings.[33]

The Open Meetings Law also gives any person the right to attend open sessions of official board meetings.[34] It does not, however, give the public a right to address the social services board or participate in the board's deliberations.[35] A social services board, though, may set aside time at meetings for comments and questions from the public if it chooses but must take any action necessary to ensure that otherwise confidential information is not improperly disclosed in connection with the public comment period.[36]

Minutes

The state's Open Meetings Law requires each county social services board to keep "full and accurate minutes" of its official meetings (including closed sessions).[37]

Because state law designates the county social services director as the board's secretary, minutes of social services board meetings should be taken by the county social services director or by a county social services employee acting under the director's supervision.[38]

Minutes of social services board meetings may be kept in written form, or, if the board chooses, in the form of sound or video and sound recordings.[39]

The purpose of taking minutes of social services board meetings is "to provide a record of the actions taken by [the] board and evidence that the [board's] actions were taken according to proper procedures."[40] At a minimum, the board's minutes must accurately reflect the substance of all official actions taken by the board and the vote by which action was taken. The board's minutes, however, need not summarize or quote each member's comments with respect to an issue, reflect the name of the member who offered a motion, or (except when the board has voted by written ballot) record the names of the members who voted for or against a motion. If the board doesn't take any action at a meeting, "no minutes (other than a record that the meeting occurred) are necessary," and if the board holds a closed session but doesn't take any action during the closed session, a statement to that effect made during the subsequent open session of the board's meeting and recorded in the minutes of the open session satisfies the legal requirements regarding minutes of closed sessions.[41]

If a social services board meets in closed session, the board must prepare a "general account of the closed session so that a person not in attendance would have a reasonable understanding of what transpired."[42] The general account of a closed session may consist of a written narrative or an audio or audiovisual recording of the session.[43]

Although state law does not explicitly require that social services boards officially approve the minutes of their meetings, it is common (and good) practice to do so. If the board determines that the proposed minutes offered by the director are incorrect or incomplete, the board may amend or correct the minutes to ensure that they are full and accurate.

The minutes (and proposed or draft minutes) of open sessions of social services board meetings are public records and must be made available for public inspection and copying under the state's Public Records Law except to the extent that they contain privileged or confidential information that is protected from public disclosure under federal or state law.[44]

The Open Meetings Law, however, permits a social services board to withhold from public inspection the minutes and general account of a closed session for "so long as public inspection would frustrate the purpose of a closed session."[45]

The social services board and director must preserve the original minutes of social services board meetings until they have no further official or historical value and are authorized to be destroyed pursuant to a records retention and disposition schedule established by the state Department of Cultural Resources and the county or until the minutes are authorized by the Department of Cultural Resources to be destroyed or transferred to the State Records Center.

Closed Sessions

The term closed session refers to the part of an official social services board meeting from which the general public and press may be lawfully excluded while the board considers particular matters. Every closed session, therefore, occurs within an official social services board meeting to which the public notice requirements of the state's Open Meetings Law apply. This means that the social services board cannot hold a secret meeting (that is, without providing public notice of the meeting in accordance with the requirements of the Open Meetings Law) even if it intends and is authorized to conduct all of its business during closed session.[46]

North Carolina's Open Meetings Law provides that a social services board may meet in closed session only upon a motion that is made by a board member, that states the purpose for holding a closed session, and that is adopted in open session by a majority of the board members present and voting.[47]

In addition, the state's Open Meetings Law provides that a social services board may meet in closed session only

- to prevent the disclosure of information that is privileged or confidential under state or federal law or is not considered to be a public record under North Carolina's public records law;[48]
- to consult with an attorney employed or retained by the social services board in order to preserve the attorney–client privilege;[49]
- to consider the qualifications, competence, performance, character, fitness, conditions of appointment, or conditions of initial employment of the county social services director or to hear or investigate a complaint, charge, or grievance by or against the county social services director or a county social services employee;[50]
- to plan, conduct, or hear reports concerning investigations of alleged criminal misconduct;[51] or
- to consider or take action with respect to other matters specified in G.S. 143-318.11.

By contrast, a social services board may not meet in closed session

- to consider issues related to general personnel policy;[52]
- to take final action to appoint or discharge the county social services director;[53]
- to consider the qualifications, competence, performance, character, fitness, appointment, or removal of a member of the county social services board;[54] or
- to discuss or evaluate the board's performance as a board.

When a social services board holds a closed session, the only persons who have a right to attend are the board members. The board, however, may allow the social services director, social services staff, or others to attend a closed session if the board chooses to do so and their presence or participation will be helpful to the board.[55] A public body, though, may not allow some people to attend a closed session while arbitrarily excluding others.[56]

When a social services board meets in closed session, it may not discuss or take action on any matter other than the matter that was specified in the motion to meet in closed session. So if the board wants to discuss another matter in closed session, it must reconvene in open session and adopt another motion to meet in closed session to discuss or act on the other matter.

Liability for Violating the Open Meetings Law

Any person who believes that the social services board has violated the state's Open Meetings Law may file a lawsuit against the board in district or superior court. If a district or superior court judge finds that the board violated the Open Meetings Law, the judge may issue a mandatory or prohibitory injunction that enjoins the board from threatened or continuing violations of the Open Meetings Law or the recurrence of past violations of the law.[57] If a superior court judge finds that the board violated the Open Meetings Law, the judge may declare any action taken by the board in violation of the law to be null and void.[58]

If the county social services board is sued for violating the state's Open Meetings Law and a superior court judge finds that the board violated the Open Meetings Law, the judge may order the board to pay the attorney's fee of the person or entity that sued the board or, if the judge finds that any board member knowingly or intentionally violated the Open Meetings Law, order that all or part of the plaintiff's attorney's fee be paid personally by that board member.[59] A judge, however, may not order an individual social services board member to pay the plaintiff's attorney's fee in a lawsuit under the state Open Meetings Law if the board member or the social services board sought and followed the advice of an attorney with respect to the board's actions.[60]

Notes

1. N.C. Gen. Stat. § 108A-7 (hereinafter G.S.).

2. North Carolina's Open Meetings Law is discussed in detail in David M. Lawrence, *Open Meetings and Local Governments in North Carolina: Some Questions and Answers* (Chapel Hill: School of Government, The University of North Carolina at Chapel Hill, 2008). The underlying principle of the Open Meetings Law is that public bodies doing the public's business should conduct their business in public. The Open Meetings Law therefore requires that public bodies give public notice of all of their meetings and that all of their meetings be open to the public unless there is specific legal authority for excluding the public from a closed session. The state Open Meetings Law applies to any state or local government board, commission, or authority that has at least two members and is authorized to exercise advisory, administrative, policy-making, quasi-judicial, or legislative authority.

3. The law, however, does not require that board meetings be held on the same day of each month or that a board meeting be held within one month of the last meeting.

4. Additional board meetings may be called by the board chair or in accordance with the board's rules of procedure. *See* G.S. 108A-7.

5. If the board chair calls an additional meeting, the board chair may specify the date, time, and location of the additional meeting.

6. *See* G.S. 143-318.12. A social services board, therefore, can never hold a secret meeting (that is, a meeting for which no public notice has been given).

7. *See* G.S. 143-318.10(d). Participating in deliberations includes not only collective discussion but also the collective acquisition and exchange of facts that a public body will consider in making a decision. A social services board cannot avoid the public notice requirements of the Open Meetings Law simply by calling a meeting a briefing session, information session, work session, or retreat. A bona fide social gathering or training session for social services board members at which no pending business of the board is discussed or transacted, however, is not an official meeting.

8. *See* G.S. 143-318.12. If the board has given proper public notice of a regular, special, or emergency meeting and then recesses during the meeting (for example, to take a break or move to another room), the board must announce the place and time for the recessed meeting, and no additional notice is required. *See* G.S. 143-318.12(b)(1). The announcement of the recessed meeting, however, may not be made while the board is holding a closed session

9. *See* G.S. 143-318.12(a). The board, of course, may provide additional public notice of its regular meetings through posted notices, flyers, mailings, radio or newspaper announcements, or other means that exceed the Open Meetings Law's requirements regarding public notice.

10. G.S. 143-318.12(a)(4).

11. *See* G.S. 143-318.12(b)(2).

12. *See* G.S. 143-318.12(b)(3). If the board holds an emergency meeting, it may not consider or act on any matter other than those matters directly related to the emergency.

13. G.S. 108A-7. *See also* G.S. 143-318.11(a)(6) (prohibiting a public body from considering the qualifications or appointment of a member of that public body during a closed session of an official meeting). Unless the board's procedures or policies provide otherwise, the board chair should be elected by a majority of the board members (including newly

appointed social services board members if they have taken their oaths of office) who are currently serving on the board and are present at the meeting. The fact that a board member has been nominated to serve as chair does not disqualify the nominee from participating in the election of the board's chair.

14. If the incumbent board chair's term on the social services board has expired and his or her successor has assumed office, the vice-chair (if the board has an incumbent vice-chair), another current board member, or the social services director (if designated by board policy or procedure) should preside at the meeting until the board elects a new board chair. If the incumbent board chair's term on the social services board has not expired, or the chair is holding over until his or her successor has assumed office, the incumbent chair should preside at the meeting until the board elects a new board chair or reelects the incumbent chair.

15. If the board has not elected a vice-chair, or if the vice-chair and the chair are both absent or unable to perform the chair's duties, the remaining board members may authorize by majority vote another board member or the county social services director to preside at a board meeting. The director, however, is not a member of the social services board even when he or she presides at a social services board meeting and may not, under any circumstance, vote with respect to matters being considered by the social services board.

16. G.S. 108A-7.

17. Any social services board member, however, may appeal the chair's decision regarding a procedural matter, and the board by majority vote may affirm or reverse the chair's decision.

18. G.S. 7B-1407(b)(6).

19. Discussions regarding the chair's performance and role may not take place during a closed session of a social services board meeting. See G.S. 143-318.11(a)(6).

20. John Carver, *Boards That Make a Difference* (San Francisco: Jossey-Bass, 2006), 258, 260.

21. While it is certainly appropriate for the board's agenda to include reports from the social services director and staff, these informational reports should not distract the board from its own work.

22. See Carver, *Boards That Make a Difference*, 19, 46, 173.

23. Once adopted, the agenda may be changed during the meeting but only by a vote of the board.

24. See G.S. 143-318.13(c).

25. The confidentiality of social services records is discussed in detail in Chapter 13 of John L. Saxon, *Social Services in North Carolina* (Chapel Hill: School of Government, The University of North Carolina at Chapel Hill, 2008).

26. See A. Fleming Bell, II, *Suggested Rules of Procedure for Small Local Government Boards* (Chapel Hill: Institute of Government, The University of North Carolina at Chapel Hill, 1998), 2.

27. Bell, *Suggested Rules of Procedure for Small Local Government Boards*. Although some social services boards adopt and try to use Roberts' Rules of Order, Roberts' rules "are not always appropriate for small governing boards" and may be "unnecessarily cumber-

some," formal, and detailed in the context of social services board meetings. Bell, *Suggested Rules of Procedure for Small Local Government Boards,* 1.

28. If board members act at a meeting at which a quorum is not present, their actions are invalid unless subsequently ratified or confirmed by the board at a meeting at which a quorum is present.

29. A county social services board could, of course, require the presence of more than a majority of the board's membership for board action (for example, all three members of a three-member board or four or five members of a five-member board), but doing so might prevent the board from acting promptly. A board also could specify that two members of a five-member board constitute a quorum, but doing so might increase the possibility of the board's taking action that is not supported by a majority of the board's members.

30. The North Carolina Attorney General has ruled that in the absence of a specific statutory authorization that allows a member of a local government board to vote by proxy, a local government board may not allow proxy voting by an absent board member. *See* 49 Op. N.C. Att'y Gen. 67 (1979).

31. *See* G.S. 143-318.13(b).

32. *See* G.S. 143-318.14(a).

33. G.S. 143-318.14(b).

34. G.S. 143-318.10(a).

35. The board chair may direct any person, including a board member, to leave a social services board meeting if the person is willfully interrupting, disrupting, or disturbing the meeting. *See* G.S. 143-318.17.

36. *See* John B. Stephens and A. Fleming Bell, II, "Public Comment at Meetings of Local Government Boards: Guidelines for Good Practices," *Popular Government* 62(4) (Summer 1997): 3; A. Fleming Bell, II, John B. Stephens, and Christopher M. Bass, "Public Comment at Meetings of Local Government Boards: Common Practices and Legal Standards," *Popular Government* 63(1) (Fall 1997): 27

37. G.S. 143-318.10(e).

38. *See* G.S. 108A-14(a)(1). If the director or the employee who has been designated to take minutes is excluded from a closed session of a board meeting, minutes of the closed session should be taken by a board member or another person designated by the board or board chair.

39. G.S. 143-318.10(e).

40. Lawrence, *Open Meetings and Local Governments in North Carolina*, 34; Maready v. City of Winston-Salem, 342 N.C. 708, 467 S.E.2d 615 (1996).

41. *Id.*

42. G.S. 143-318.10(e); Multimedia Publ'g of N.C., Inc. v. Henderson County, 145 N.C. App. 365, 550 S.E.2d 846 (2001). The board must prepare an account of a closed session even if minutes of the closed session are not required. Lawrence, *Open Meetings and Local Governments in North Carolina*, 34.

43. G.S. 143-318.10(e).

44. *Id.*

45. *Id.*

46. Lawrence, *Open Meetings and Local Governments in North Carolina*, 17.

47. G.S. 143-318.11(c).

48. G.S. 143-318.11(a)(1). *See also* G.S. 108A-80 (providing that records of persons who have applied for or received public assistance or social services from a county social services department are confidential). When the board meets in closed session to prevent the disclosure of confidential information, the motion to meet in closed session must state the name or citation of the law that renders the information privileged or confidential. G.S. 143-318.11(c).

49. G.S. 143-318.11(a)(3). The fact that an attorney retained or employed by a social services board participates in a board meeting does not in and of itself justify holding a closed session. Nor may a social services board meet in closed session to discuss general policy matters with an attorney. If the board holds a closed session to discuss pending litigation with an attorney, the motion to meet in closed session must identify the parties to the litigation. When meeting in closed session under this provision, a social services board may give instructions to the attorney concerning the handling or settlement of a claim, judicial action, mediation, arbitration, or administrative procedure. If, however, the board considers or approves the settlement of a claim or legal proceeding in closed session, the terms of the settlement must be reported to the board and entered into its minutes as soon as possible within a reasonable time after the settlement is concluded.

50. G.S. 143-318.11(a)(6).

51. G.S. 143-318.11(a)(7).

52. G.S. 143-318.11(a)(6).

53. *Id.* The board, however, may reach tentative consensus during a closed session with respect to the appointment or discharge of the county social services director and then take formal action in open session to appoint or discharge the director. *See* Maready v. City of Winston-Salem, 342 N.C. 708, 467 S.E.2d 615 (1996).

54. G.S. 143-318.11(a)(6).

55. A public body must be particularly careful in deciding who will be allowed to attend a closed session held to preserve the attorney–client privilege because the presence of persons other than the members of the public body and the body's attorney may destroy the privileged nature of the discussion.

56. If the social services board lawfully excludes a person from a closed session of a board meeting and the person refuses to leave, he or she may be prosecuted for criminal trespass under G.S. 14-159.13.

57. G.S. 143-318.16.

58. G.S. 143-318.16A.

59. G.S. 143-318.16B.

60. *Id.*

Chapter 11

Working Together to Improve the Board's Effectiveness

Working Together as a Board

The county social services board is a public body. It is a group of individuals that is created by law to work together for a particular purpose and to achieve a common goal.

Each individual appointed to the social services board brings to the board his or her unique personality, life experience, communication style, talents, vision, beliefs, and perspectives. And each person who serves on the social services board is a public official and is individually accountable to the public for his or her service as a board member.

Board members are individuals. But they are also members of the board and need to work together to fulfill both their individual responsibilities as public officials and the board's responsibilities as a public body.

This doesn't mean that board members will always agree with each other or that there will never be differences of opinion or conflicts among board members. What it means is that board members need to create ways of working together that respect individual differences, ensure good communication, resolve conflicts constructively, improve the board's effectiveness and performance, and achieve the purposes for which the board was created.

Characteristics of Effective Boards

According to John Carver, the role of the governing board of a government agency or nonprofit organization is to

- provide visionary leadership for the agency or organization;
- articulate the agency's or organization's mission, goals, objectives, and core values;
- act as trustee for and be accountable to the agency's or organization's "moral owners;"
- empower the director and staff of the agency or organization to carry out the agency's or organization's mission;
- specify the limitations within which the director and staff must act;
- monitor and evaluate the agency's or organization's performance in meeting its mission, goals, and objectives; and
- monitor and evaluate the board's own performance.[1]

And, Carver writes, to do these things effectively, a governing board must

- focus on the future rather than the past or present;
- have a long-term, not short-term, perspective;
- adopt an outward, not inward, focus;
- act proactively rather than reactively;
- act independently but cooperatively;
- focus its attention on the big picture rather than the details;
- focus on outcomes and impacts rather than procedures and processes;
- understand, differentiate, and clarify if necessary the roles and authority of the board and the director; and
- refrain from trying to micromanage the work of the director and staff.[2]

Improving the Board's Effectiveness

There are several ways of defining what it means for a board, group, or team to be successful or effective.

One definition of group effectiveness suggests that a group is effective or successful if

- the group's work (delivering a product or service) meets or exceeds the standard specified for acceptable or satisfactory performance,

- the group functions in a way that maintains or enhances the ability of its members to work together, and
- the group experience satisfies rather than frustrates the personal needs of group members.[3]

Using this definition, Margaret Carlson identifies three variables that can positively or negatively affect a group's success or effectiveness:

- organizational context,
- group structure, and
- group process.[4]

The organizational context of county social services boards consists of the aspects of the larger governmental, political, cultural, social, and economic systems in which social services boards function. Social services boards do not exist in a vacuum. As local government boards, their powers and duties are defined and limited by state law. Their authority to establish social services policy is significantly limited by state and federal law. And their ability to influence the response of state and local governments to the social and economic problems of their communities often is limited by political, financial, social, and economic realities. All of these factors can affect the ability of county social services boards to function effectively or achieve their goals. And all of these factors are in large part beyond their direct control.

There are, however, several ways in which social services boards can seek to influence and change the organizational context in which they exist. If, for example, a social services board needs information, training, support, or other resources and cannot obtain those things on its own, it should seek them from the social services director, state social services employees, the board of county commissioners, other public agencies, or other sources. And because a supportive organizational culture increases the chances of success for a group that exists within a larger organization, social services boards should identify the values and beliefs of the social services director, the county manager, county commissioners, the general public, and others who may impact the board's work and, if those values and beliefs negatively impact the board's work, seek to change them.

"Group structure" refers to the "relatively stable characteristics of a group," such as the group's membership, its task, and the ways its members interact.[5] Like organizational context, the structure of a group may positively or negatively affect its ability to work effectively and achieve its goals.

Some aspects of a group's structure are within the group's control. A group, for example, can build a structure that supports the group's work by establishing clear goals based on a shared understanding of and commitment to the group's mission and purpose; identifying specific tasks that will motivate and involve group members to use their time, energy, and skills to achieve the goals; clearly articulating the roles and responsibilities of members; setting aside sufficient time to accomplish the group's work; and creating a culture, norms, and procedures that support the group's ability to work together effectively.[6]

Other aspects of a group's structure, however, may be beyond a group's direct control. A social services board, for example, doesn't have the authority to determine the board's size or who (other than the third board member) will be appointed to the board. But it can help shape its structure by encouraging the state Social Services Commission and county commissioners to make appointments to the board in a way that ensures that the board will consist of members who have the right mix of knowledge, experience, and skills to accomplish the board's work.

The third variable that may affect a group's effectiveness is the group's process. A group's process and structure are closely related. For example, the culture and norms that a group establishes either explicitly or implicitly will almost always shape the ways that group members work together and relate to each other. Group structure, however, refers primarily to the what and the who of a group while group process refers to how a group makes decisions, attempts to solve problems, handles disagreements and conflict, communicates, shares information, and sets boundaries that manage its relationship with its external environment.[7]

There is, of course, no single right way for a group to make decisions, solve problems, handle conflicts, share information, communicate, or set boundaries. Most groups, however, have a great deal of authority to shape, and change if necessary, their own internal processes in ways that can improve their effectiveness.

Social services boards, therefore, should first identify and discuss the ways that board members make decisions, discuss problems, share information, communicate with each other, and handle disagreements. Then board members should explore, with each other and the social services director, ways in which their processes for making decisions, discussing problems, managing conflict, and working together might be improved.

Groups, for example, "often encounter difficulties when they are attempting to solve problems."[8] Sometimes group members "begin discussing possible solutions before agreeing on the nature of a problem," or some members are "debating the cause of the problem while others are evaluating possible" solutions.[9] A social services board, therefore, might improve its ability to solve problems or make decisions by adopting and following an explicit and systematic process for identifying problems, determining the causes of those problems, agreeing on the criteria for acceptable solutions, generating potential solutions, agreeing on and implementing solutions, and evaluating the results of implementing those solutions.[10]

Good communication among board members is essential for the board's success. "To solve problems effectively, a group must have valid information," and to generate valid information, group members must share relevant information with each other "in a way that enables other members to determine for themselves whether the information is valid" and then make free and informed choices.[11] Poor communication, on the other hand, undermines the ability of board members to work together. According to Carlson, "Many communication problems occur in groups because people misunderstand other members' verbal and nonverbal messages, fail to check whether they have correctly interpreted the message, and then respond on the basis of their untested inferences."[12] Other problems arise when group members fail to treat other members with respect, deal with group conflict or differences of opinion in ways that aren't healthy or productive, or avoid conflict by refusing to discuss "undiscussable" issues.

A social services board, therefore, can improve its effectiveness by adopting and following ground rules that encourage board members to

- share all information (including feelings, opinions, and facts that don't support one's own position or interest) that might affect the way the board makes a decision;
- test the assumptions and inferences they make before reacting to what someone else has said or done;
- focus on their interests, needs, desires, and concerns with respect to issues rather than particular positions or solutions;
- be specific and use examples when speaking rather than making general, broad, or vague statements;
- agree on the meaning of important words;
- explain the reasons behind one's statements, questions, and actions;

- invite others to comment, disagree, or ask questions in response to one's statements or ideas;
- disagree openly, but politely and respectfully, with others;
- discuss "undiscussable" issues;
- stay focused on the issue, problem, or discussion that is before the board;
- refrain from taking cheap shots at others or engaging in any behavior that distracts the board from its work; and
- allow all board members to participate fully in the board's discussion, decisions, and work.[13]

Using Carlson's model for improving a group's effectiveness, social services boards that are interested in improving their effectiveness should

- understand the organizational context and culture within which they function and work to create good relationships with local government officials, state social services agencies, businesses, churches, nonprofit agencies, community organizations, and the public;
- seek the information, training, support, and resources they need from other public agencies and officials;
- establish clear goals for the board based on a shared understanding of and commitment to the board's mission and purpose;
- identify specific tasks to motivate and involve board members to use their time, energy, and skills to achieve the board's goals;
- understand and clearly articulate the roles and responsibilities of board members;
- set aside sufficient time to accomplish the board's work;
- identify and discuss the board's culture and explicit or implicit norms and decide whether changing the board's culture or norms would improve effectiveness;
- develop and follow a decision-making process that ensures that decisions are based on valid information, careful deliberation, and free and open participation by all board members;
- use a problem-solving process that identifies particular problems, determines their causes, establishes criteria for acceptable solutions, generates potential solutions, selects specific solutions, implements those solutions, and evaluates the results of those solutions;

- recognize and respond to conflict and diversity among board members in creative and productive ways; and
- establish and follow ground rules to encourage better communication among board members.

Evaluating the Board's Work

Another way that a county social services board can improve its effectiveness is to evaluate the board's work and performance on a regular basis.

A social services board's self-evaluation process should measure both the board's process (that is, how the board functions) and the board's "product" (that is, the actual results or impacts the board has achieved).

To evaluate the board's product, the board must first define the nature and scope of its responsibilities as a board. In doing so, board members should be careful to distinguish between the board's work or responsibilities and the work or responsibilities of the social services department, director, and employees. Board members, therefore, should develop a job description for the board and use the description as the basis for the board's self-evaluation. The board's job description should, of course, include all the board's legal responsibilities specified by state law. But the legal responsibilities are only a starting point. Because the board's job, broadly defined, is governance, the board's job description should focus on the entire range of the board's work. In addition the board should consider any specific goals or objectives it has set for itself regarding its work.

A social services board's evaluation of its work, therefore, might focus on several broad areas, including

- the extent to which the board provides effective leadership and oversight for the social services department;
- the board's relationship with the county social services director;
- the way in which the board conducts its business at board meetings and works together;
- the board's awareness of social conditions and problems in the community; and
- the ways in which the board interacts with state and county officials, public and private agencies, and the public.

Within each of these broad areas, the board might identify several specific tasks or elements of the board's work or process that should be considered. For example, within the general area of the board's relationship with the director, a board might evaluate whether it has clearly communicated its expectations and concerns to the director, whether it has established clear standards and a fair and effective process for evaluating the director's performance, and whether the board has refrained from infringing on the director's administrative authority. Or in the general area of the board's process, board members might consider whether the board has established and follows rules of procedure for board meetings, whether necessary information is provided to board members before each meeting, whether board meetings start and end on time and the board maintains adequate minutes, and whether board members exercise good listening skills and treat each other, the director, the staff, and the public with respect.[14]

After a board has identified the specific elements of its work that it wants to evaluate, board members must agree on how the board's performance regarding each specific task will be measured or the criteria against which the board's performance will be assessed.[15] In some instances the board may be able to establish an objective, quantifiable standard against which its performance can be measured. In other instances a board may assess its performance through a somewhat more subjective process in which board members conclude that the board's performance is satisfactory or needs improvement or that rates the board's performance on a scale of one to ten. In either case, though, board members should agree not only about what aspects of the board's work will be evaluated but also how the board's work will be evaluated.

Next the board should agree on a process and time frame for completing its evaluation. One approach might be for each board member to complete the self-evaluation form developed by the board and then for board members to compare and discuss their individual evaluations of the board's performance and attempt to arrive at a consensus on the board's performance in each area of its work.[16] The final and most important step in a board's self-evaluation, however, is identifying the areas in which the board's performance is less than satisfactory or needs improvement, developing an action plan to address the most important areas in which deficiencies were noted, implementing the plan, and regularly reviewing the board's progress in addressing issues identified in the plan.

Evaluating the board's performance takes time, understanding, and commitment as well as trust, good faith, sensitivity, and respect for one's fellow board members. If a board's self-evaluation is based on these underlying values and commitments and board members focus on improving the board's performance rather than criticizing or pointing fingers at others, the board can make the self-evaluation process one of its most productive and rewarding activities.

Notes

1. *See* John Carver, *Boards That Make a Difference* (San Francisco: Jossey-Bass, 2006).

2. *Id*

3. *See* Margaret S. Carlson, "A Model for Improving a Group's Effectiveness," *Popular Government* 63(4) (Summer 1998): 37.

4. *Id.*

5. *Id* at 40.

6. Group culture refers to the set of shared values and beliefs that guide the behavior of group members. Group norms are specific expectations about how group members should or should not behave. They are shared by all or many group members and are closely linked to the group's culture. Often group norms are implicit (or unstated) rather than explicit. *Id*. at 41–42.

7. *Id*

8. *Id*. at 42.

9. Carlson, "A Model for Improving a Group's Effectiveness," 42.

10. *Id*

11. Roger M. Schwarz, *Ground Rules for Effective Groups* (Chapel Hill: Institute of Government, The University of North Carolina at Chapel Hill, 1994).

12. Carlson, "A Model for Improving a Group's Effectiveness," 42–43.

13. *See* Schwarz, *Ground Rules for Effective Groups*.

14. Although a board may ask each of its members to evaluate his or her performance as a social services board member, the focus of the board's self-evaluation should be the board's performance as a group, not as individuals.

15. If measurement criteria for performance do not exist, the board should clarify its expectations with a statement describing "what success would look like" or the desired result or outcome.

16. Unlike the board's discussion of the director's performance, discussions regarding the board's performance may not take place during a closed session of a social services board meeting. The state's Open Meetings Law is discussed in Chapter 10 of this handbook.

Chapter 12

Legal Liability and Immunity of the Social Services Board and Board Members

Although county social services board members sometimes worry about the possibility that they will be sued or held liable in connection with their actions as public officials, social services board members rarely are sued or prosecuted in connection with their service on the board and seldom are held legally liable for their actions as board members.[1]

Liability in "Official Capacity" Lawsuits

A civil lawsuit that claims the county social services board acted unlawfully in the course of performing its official duties and is filed against the board or board members in their official capacities is called an official capacity lawsuit. When a person files an official capacity lawsuit and seeks monetary damages based on the board's alleged violation of state or federal laws, the lawsuit is, in essence, a lawsuit against the county—not a lawsuit against the individual social services board members. This means that if a monetary judgment is entered against the social services board or board members in their official capacities, the legal liability and responsibility for paying the judgment lie with the county and not with the social services board members as individuals.

Although official capacity lawsuits against county social services boards are rare, they sometimes are filed in response to the board's alleged violation of the State Personnel Act or federal employment discrimination statutes in connection with the board's appointment or dismissal of the county social services director.

If an official capacity lawsuit is filed against the social services board or board members, the board should immediately contact the county attorney and follow the attorney's instructions regarding the lawsuit.[2]

Board Members' Liability Under 42 U.S.C. 1983

42 U.S.C. 1983 ("section 1983") is a federal statute that authorizes a person to sue and receive injunctive relief or monetary damages from a local government or local government official if the government's or official's conduct violates the person's legal rights under the United States Constitution or certain federal statutes.[3]

State and county social services agencies were sued frequently under this statute during the 1960s, 1970s, and 1980s by persons who had applied for or were receiving public assistance or social services and alleged that the agencies had violated the plaintiffs' legal rights by failing to comply with the requirements of the federal Social Security Act or other federal social services statutes.[4] Recent decisions of the U.S. Supreme Court, however, have limited somewhat the ability of social services clients and others to bring section 1983 lawsuits against state and county social services agencies for alleged violations of federal social services statutes.[5]

State and county social services agencies, officials, and employees may be sued for prospective injunctive relief under section 1983, and counties may be held liable for monetary damages in section 1983 lawsuits that involve the conduct of county social services officials or employees.[6]

In addition, social services board members may be held personally liable for monetary damages under section 1983 when sued in their "individual capacities." They are entitled, however, to a qualified immunity that protects them from personal liability unless their conduct "violates clearly established statutory or constitutional rights about which a reasonable person in similar circumstances would have known."[7]

County social services board members, therefore, may be held liable under 42 U.S.C. 1983 if their actions violate the federal constitutional or statutory rights of an individual. Board members, however, are rarely sued and have rarely, if ever, been held individually liable under section 1983.[8]

Liability Under the Open Meetings Law

Anyone who believes that the social services board has violated the state's Open Meetings Law may file a lawsuit against the board in district or superior court. If a district or superior court judge finds that the board violated the Open Meetings Law, the judge may issue a mandatory or prohibitory injunction that enjoins the board from threatened or continuing violations of the Open Meetings Law or the recurrence of past violations of the law.[9] If a superior court judge finds that the board violated the Open Meetings Law, the judge may declare any action taken by the board in violation of the law to be null and void.[10]

A judge may not enter a monetary judgment against the county social services board or board members based on the board's violation of the Open Meetings Law. But if the board is sued for violating the Open Meetings Law and a superior court judge finds that the board violated that law, the judge may order the board to pay the attorney's fee of the person or entity that sued the board or, if the judge finds that any board member knowingly or intentionally violated the Open Meetings Law, order that all or part of the plaintiff's attorney's fee be paid personally by that board member.[11] A judge, however, may not order an individual social services board member to pay the plaintiff's attorney's fee in a lawsuit under the state Open Meetings Law if the board member or the social services board sought and followed the advice of an attorney regarding the board's actions.[12]

Board Members' Liability and Immunity for Torts

A tort is a wrongful act or omission, other than a criminal act or breach of contract, that causes personal injury or damage to property and with respect to which the law provides a legal cause of action and a legal remedy.

> Compensation is the primary concern of tort law. This area of law is premised on the belief that individuals who [have been harmed by the wrongful conduct of others] . . . should not be required to bear the loss; instead, the person

whose wrongful act caused the harm must pay to restore the injured party to where [he or she] . . . was before the harm. Another purpose of tort law is to deter people from engaging in conduct likely to cause personal injury or property damage. Tort law assumes that people will be more careful in conducting their day-to-day activities if they have to pay for any harm that results.[13]

Tort law, therefore, serves to protect a person's interest in his or her bodily security, tangible property, financial resources, or reputation. Unlike contract law, in which the appropriate standard of conduct is set by specific promises made between two parties, in tort law individuals are held to a standard of conduct (or duty) imposed by law. To succeed in a tort lawsuit, the injured party (the plaintiff) must demonstrate that the person against whom the tort claim is brought (the defendant) violated that duty and that the violation caused an injury to the plaintiff or the plaintiff's property.

If a defendant is found liable in connection with a tort claim, a judgment for monetary damages may be entered against him or her. In most cases the damages awarded in tort claims are compensatory damages (damages awarded to compensate the plaintiff for his or her physical injury, the damage to his or her property, incurred medical expenses, lost future earnings, pain and suffering, or other losses). Courts sometimes award punitive damages against a defendant in order to "punish [the] defendant for especially culpable conduct and to deter such conduct in the future."[14] Punitive damages, however, "generally are not recoverable from a governmental body or agency," though they may be assessed against a "public employee or official in an 'individual-capacity' lawsuit."[15]

There are two broad categories of torts: intentional torts and unintentional torts (negligence).

"Intentional torts are deliberate wrongful acts that cause personal injury or property damage."[16] A defendant may be held liable for an intentional tort if he or she "deliberately engaged in the wrongful act" regardless of whether he or she "intended the consequences of the act [or] . . . the particular damages caused."[17] The tort of battery, which the law defines as the "intentional touching or striking of another person without . . . that person's consent or a legally recognized authorization," is one example of an intentional tort.[18] Defamation (slander or libel) is another.

By contrast, a defendant may be held civilly liable for negligence if

- the defendant breaches his or her legal duty to exercise reasonable care in connection with his or her activities;

- the defendant's failure to exercise reasonable care results in injury to another person or that person's property; and
- the injury was a reasonably foreseeable result of the defendant's lack of care.[19]

For example, a person whose failure to exercise reasonable care and attention in driving his or her automobile results in an accident may be liable for his or her negligence.

A person who has been injured by the allegedly tortious conduct of a social services board member while the board member was engaged in his or her official duties may sue the member in his or her individual capacity.[20] When a lawsuit is filed against a social services board member in his or her individual capacity, the plaintiff is asking the court to hold the board member personally liable for the damages the plaintiff has suffered.[21]

It is not always easy to determine, however, whether a public official or employee is being sued in his or her individual capacity, in his or her official capacity, or in both capacities.

> The crucial question for determining whether a [public official or employee] . . . is sued in an individual or official capacity is the nature of the relief sought, not the nature of the act or omission alleged. If the plaintiff seeks an injunction requiring the defendant to take an action involving the exercise of a government power, the defendant is [sued] . . . in an official capacity. If money damages are sought, the court must ascertain whether the complaint indicates that the damages are sought from the government or from the pocket of the individual defendant. If the former, it is an official-capacity claim; if the latter, it is an individual-capacity claim; and if it is both, then the claims proceed in both capacities.[22]
>
> In ascertaining the capacity in which the plaintiff seeks to sue [a public official or employee] . . . , the court will typically look first to the caption of the complaint [which should indicate the capacity or capacities in which the defendant is being sued]. If the [caption doesn't clearly indicate the capacity in which the defendant is being sued] . . . , the court will look to the allegations of the complaint and then to the course of the proceedings. Absent some clear indication in the allegations or the procedural history of the case, the court will not presume that the plaintiff sought to impose personal liability on the defendant. Instead the presumption will operate in favor of finding only official-capacity liability.[23]

Social services board members are not entitled to governmental immunity when sued in their individual, rather than official, capacities.[24] They are, however, protected by a limited immunity when sued in their individual capacities for alleged negligence.[25]

This public official immunity protects a social services board member from personal liability for his or her alleged negligence in "the exercise of a discretionary act while engaged in a governmental activity, unless [he or she] acted with malice, for corrupt reasons, or outside the scope of his or her official duties."[26] But it is not complete or absolute. It does not, for example, protect a social services board member whose negligence in driving an automobile to a social services board meeting results in an accident. Nor does it protect a board member who is sued in his or her individual capacity for committing an intentional tort.[27] And it does not protect a board member if he or she is sued for allegedly violating a person's rights under the U.S. Constitution or federal law.[28]

Criminal Liability of Social Services Board Members

Criminal liability results from a person's violation of federal or state criminal laws. A person who is charged with a criminal offense generally may be arrested for that offense and, if he or she pleads guilty or is tried and convicted of the crime charged, be punished by incarceration in jail or prison, by being placed on probation, or by being ordered to pay a fine.

County social services board members are subject to the general criminal laws of North Carolina and the United States as well as to particular criminal laws that govern the conduct of public officials. This means that a county social services board member may be charged with, arrested for, tried for, and, if convicted, punished for a criminal offense that he or she commits in connection with his or her service on the county social services board, such as

- unlawfully disclosing confidential information regarding persons who have applied for or are receiving public assistance or social services from the county social services department;[29]
- unlawfully receiving a direct benefit from a contract that involves the county social services department or receiving a gift in return for attempting to influence the award of a contract by the county social services department;[30]

- disrupting an official meeting of the county social services board or another public body;[31]
- threatening or assaulting other social services board members, the county social services director, other public officials or employees, or other persons;
- embezzling or misapplying county property or funds;[32] or
- willfully failing to discharge his or her duties as a social services board member.[33]

Legal Representation and Indemnification of Board Members

A county may, upon the request of a county social services board member, provide legal representation for the board member in connection with any civil or criminal action brought against the board member in state or federal court on account of alleged acts or omissions committed in the scope and course of the board member's service as a public official.[34] This means that a county may retain and pay an attorney to represent a board member who is

- charged with a criminal offense in connection with his or her service as a social services board member, or
- sued in his or her individual capacity in a civil lawsuit that involves his or her service as a social services board member.

The county, however, is not required to do so and, if it does not, the board member is responsible for retaining and paying an attorney to represent him or her in the pending legal action.

State law also authorizes "counties . . . to purchase insurance to protect themselves and any of their officers, agents, or employees from civil liability for damages."[35] The board of county commissioners, however, "has absolute discretion in deciding which liabilities and which . . . [county officials and employees], if any, will be covered by this insurance" and in deciding whether it will cover claims under federal, as well as state, law and cover claims against officials and employees in their individual, as well as official, capacities.[36] Counties, therefore, may purchase insurance to protect county social services board members from individual liability in connection with their service as public officials. But counties are not required to purchase such insurance.

In addition, state law authorizes a county to pay all or part of any settlement or judgment entered in a lawsuit brought against a current or former county social services board member in the board member's individual capacity for an act committed within the scope of the board member's public office if

- the county has adopted a set of uniform standards under which settlements or judgments against county officials will be paid;
- the board member notifies the county of the legal claim or pending lawsuit; and
- the board of commissioners determines that the board member did not act or fail to act because of fraud, corruption, or malice.[37]

Notes

1. The legal liability and immunity of state and county social services agencies, officials, and employees is discussed in more detail in Chapter 14 of John L. Saxon, *Social Services in North Carolina* (Chapel Hill: School of Government, The University of North Carolina at Chapel Hill, 2008). The legal liability of North Carolina local governments and local government officials and employees is discussed further in Anita R. Brown-Graham, *A Practical Guide to the Liability of North Carolina Cities and Towns* (Chapel Hill: Institute of Government: The University of North Carolina at Chapel Hill, 1999); and Anita R. Brown-Graham, "Civil Liability of the Local Government and Its Officials and Employees," in *County and Municipal Government in North Carolina*, ed. David M. Lawrence (Chapel Hill: School of Government, The University of North Carolina at Chapel Hill, 2007), *available* at www.sog.unc.edu/pubs/cmg/cmg12.pdf.

2. Tort claims against social services officials or employees in their official capacities are discussed in more detail in Chapter 14 of Saxon, *Social Services in North Carolina*.

3. The liability of local governments and local government employees under this statute (section 1983) is discussed in detail in Chapter 6, Chapter 7, Chapter 8, and Chapter 10 of Brown-Graham, *A Practical Guide to Liability for North Carolina Cities and Counties*, and in Brown-Graham, "Civil Liability of the Local Government and Its Officials and Employees," 14–18.

4. *See* King v. Smith, 392 U.S. 309 (1968); Shapiro v. Thompson, 394 U.S. 618 (1969); Rosado v. Wyman, 397 U.S. 397 (1970); Lewis v. Martin, 397 U.S. 552 (1970); Wyman v. James, 400 U.S. 309 (1971); Townsend v. Swank, 404 U.S. 282 (1971); Jefferson v. Hackney, 406 U.S. 535 (1972); Carleson v. Remillard, 406 U.S. 598 (1972); New York State Dep't of Social Servs. v. Dublino, 413 U.S. 405 (1973); U.S. Dep't of Agric. v. Moreno, 413 U.S. 528 (1973); Maine v. Thiboutot, 448 U.S. 1 (1980). Legal aid attorneys have filed a number of section 1983 lawsuits against North Carolina social services agencies. See Carter v. Morrow, 526 F. Supp. 1225 (W.D.N.C. 1981) (denial of child support enforcement services); Alexander v. Hill, 549 F. Supp. 1355 (W.D.N.C. 1982) (failure to process Medicaid applications in a timely manner); Morris v. Morrow, 783 F.2d 454 (4th Cir. 1986) (Medicaid eligibility rules); Wilson v. Lyng, 662 F. Supp. 1391 (E.D.N.C. 1987) (food stamp eligibility rules); Warren v. N.C. Dep't of Human Res., 65 F.3d 385 (4th Cir. 1995) (food stamp eligibility rules).

5. *See* Deshaney v. Winnebago County Dep't of Social Servs., 489 U.S. 189 (1989); Suter v. Artist M., 503 U.S. 347 (1992) (child welfare services); Blessing v. Freestone, 520 U.S. 329 (1997) (child support enforcement services).

6. *See* Monell v. New York City Dep't of Social Servs., 436 U.S. 658 (1978). Local governments are not liable for punitive damages in section 1983 lawsuits. City of Newport v. Fact Concerts, Inc., 453 U.S. 247 (1981). State and county social services agencies and employees also may be liable for paying a plaintiff's attorneys fees in a section 1983 lawsuit. Brown-Graham, *A Practical Guide to Liability for North Carolina Cities and Counties*, 10-5 through 10-6.

7. Brown-Graham, "Civil Liability of the Local Government and Its Officials and Employees," 18, *citing* Wood v. Strickland, 420 U.S. 308 (1975) and Anderson v. Creighton, 483 U.S. 635 (1987). Punitive damages may be awarded against a county social services employee if he or she is held personally liable under section 1983, and the court finds that his or her conduct was reckless or deliberately indifferent to the plaintiff's legal rights. Smith v. Wade, 461 U.S. 30 (1983).

8. *See* Fracaro v. Priddy, 514 F. Supp. 191 (M.D.N.C. 1981); Alexander v. Hill, 549 F. Supp. 1355 (W.D.N.C. 1982).

9. N.C. Gen. Stat. § 143-318.16 (hereinafter G.S.).

10. G.S. 143-318.16A.

11. G.S. 143-318.16B.

12. *Id.*

13. Brown-Graham, "Civil Liability of the Local Government and Its Officials and Employees," 2.

14. Brown-Graham, *A Practical Guide to the Liability of North Carolina Cities and Counties*, 5-5, citing Jones v. McCaskill, 99 N.C. App. 764, 394 S.E.2d 254 (1990).

15. Brown-Graham, *A Practical Guide to the Liability of North Carolina Cities and Counties*, 5-6.

16. Brown-Graham, "Civil Liability of the Local Government and Its Officials and Employees," 3.

17. *Id.*

18. *Id.*

19. *Id.* at 4. In North Carolina a defendant may avoid liability for his or her negligent acts or omissions by proving that the plaintiff's injuries were caused in part by the plaintiff's "contributory negligence."

20. *See* Meyer v. Walls, 347 N.C. at 110, 489 S.E.2d at 887. *Cf.* McCarn v. Beach, 128 N.C. App. 435, 496 S.E.2d 402 (1998). A county social services board member also may be sued in his or her official capacity or in his or her official and individual capacities as the result of his or her allegedly tortious conduct.

21. *See* Hare v. Butler, 99 N.C. App. 693, 700, 394 S.E.2d 231, 236; Meyer v. Walls, 347 N.C. 99, 110, 489 S.E.2d 880, 887.

22. Meyer v. Walls, 347 N.C. at 110, 489 S.E.2d at 887.

23. Brown-Graham, *A Practical Guide to Liability for North Carolina Cities and Counties*, 4-5.

24. *Id.* at 4-7. *Cf.* Cherry v. Harris, 110 N.C. App. 478, 480, 429 S.E.2d 771, 772 (1993). Governmental immunity of counties and county agencies is also discussed in Chapter 14 of Saxon, *Social Services in North Carolina.*

25. County social services board members also may be immune from tort liability with respect to any "quasi-legislative" or "quasi-judicial" functions of the social services board. *See* Vereen v. Holden, 121 N.C. App. 779, 468 S.E.2d 471 (1996); Fuquay Springs v. Rowland, 239 N.C. 299, 79 S.E.2d 774 (1954).

26. Brown-Graham, *A Practical Guide to Liability for North Carolina Cities and Counties,* 4-8, *citing* Wiggins v. City of Monroe, 73 N.C. App. 44, 49, 326 S.E.2d 39, 43 (1985). A "discretionary" act is one that requires personal deliberation, decision, and judgment, contrasted with a "ministerial" act that is "absolute, certain, and imperative, and involve[s] merely the execution of a specific duty arising from fixed and designated facts." Brown-Graham, *A Practical Guide to Liability for North Carolina Cities and Counties,* 4-8, *citing* Hare v. Butler, 99 N.C. App. at 700, 394 S.E.2d at 236.

27. A social services board member, however, may assert a separate, limited immunity if he or she is sued for defamation and his or her conduct that was not malicious. *See* Brown-Graham, "Civil Liability of the Local Government and Its Officials and Employees," 4.

28. The liability and limited immunity of local government officials in connection with lawsuits under 42 U.S.C. 1983 is discussed in detail in Chapter 6, Chapter 7, Chapter 8, and Chapter 10 of Brown-Graham, *A Practical Guide to Liability for North Carolina Cities and Counties,* in Brown-Graham, "Civil Liability of the Local Government and Its Officials and Employees," 14–18, and in Chapter 14 of Saxon, *Social Services in North Carolina.*

29. G.S. 108A-80.

30. G.S. 14-234. The state's conflict of interest rules regarding public contracts are discussed in more detail in Chapter 6 of this handbook.

31. G.S. 143-318.17.

32. G.S. 14-92.

33. G.S. 14-230.

34. *See* G.S. 160A-167(a) and G.S. 153A-97.

35. Brown-Graham, "Civil Liability of the Local Government and Its Officials and Employees," 18. *See* G.S. 160A-485.

36. Brown-Graham, "Civil Liability of the Local Government and Its Officials and Employees," 18.

37. G.S. 160A-167(b).